Payne's
DEVON

First published in Great Britain in 1986 by Devon Books

Copyright © 1986 Peter Hunt
Illustrations © 1986 Devon County Council

ISBN 0 86114-790-1

British Library Cataloguing-in-Publication Data
Hunt, P. J. (Peter John)
  Payne's Devon: a portrait of the county from 1790
  to 1830 through the watercolours of William Payne.

  1. Payne, William, *s. l. 1776–1809*
  2. Devon in art
  I. Title
  II. Payne, William, *fl. 1776–1809*
  759.2   ND1942.P3/

Printed in Great Britain by A. Wheaton & Co. Ltd.

DEVON BOOKS
Official Publisher to Devon County Council
Devon Books is a division of A. Wheaton & Co. Ltd, which represents:

Editorial, Design, Publicity, Production and Manufacturing
A. Wheaton & Co. Ltd
Hennock Road, Marsh Barton, Exeter, Devon EX2 8RP
Tel: 0392 74121; Telex 42749 (WHEATN G)
(A. Wheaton & Co. Ltd is a member of the
Pergamon/B.P.C.C. Group of Companies)

Sales and Distribution
Town & Country Books, P.O. Box 31, Newton Abbot, Devon TQ12 5AQ
Tel: 080 47 2690

ACKNOWLEDGEMENTS
I am very grateful to Miss Alison Shute, County Librarian, and Mr Ian Maxted, of the West Country Studies Library, for making the original watercolours available, and to the staff of the West Country Studies Library and to the County Archivist, Mrs Margery Rowe, and the staff of the Records Office for their help. Mr Graham Ward of the County Council's Property Department was responsible for photographic reproduction of the paintings and Mr Roger Barons for proof reading. Grateful thanks also to Mrs Mary Mears of Wheatons for reading, correcting and editing the final draft.

Payne's DEVON

A Portrait of the County from 1790 to 1830
through the Watercolours of William Payne

PETER HUNT

DEVON BOOKS

List of Illustrations

Note The captions printed in this book are taken from the titles Payne wrote beneath the pictures, complete with his sometimes eccentric spelling.

Contents

Butt's Head nr St Budeaux

Introduction

Between 1790 and 1820, when William Payne was achieving considerable success as an artist and teacher, the effects of the French Revolution and war with France, together with the American War of Independence, helped to create changes to society which cast aside the limitations of earlier beliefs, social organization and ways of work. The Napoleonic Wars were the fulcrum of change from the relatively static society of earlier times to the more dynamic one where changes have been taking place with increasing speed ever since. However important developments within the past two centuries may seem, the effects of wars and the industrial revolution which took place at the start of this era were immense.

Wars that have involved the sustained effort of the whole nation have always created change, and the Napoleonic Wars led directly to technological advances in ship design and construction, such as the centre-board, first tried on the cutter *Trial* in 1790. There were also agricultural innovations such as new types of plough and seed drills, whilst machinery increased production from woollen-mills, and roads were improved as a necessary adjunct to a more mobile and enquiring society.

Almost every aspect of life was changing, with a greatly increased population which during the first half of the nineteenth century almost doubled the size of many towns and villages. Devon's popularity with visitors and attraction for retirement also increased as the roads got better, and the establishment of the tourist trade was completed with the arrival of the railway at Exeter in 1844.

In many respects Devon's society mirrored that of the country as a whole. Discrepancy of wealth and a corrupt political structure were the basis of its organization, which was increasingly being challenged, not least by the example of the French. Rotten boroughs like Honiton, with a small elite franchise, returned members to Parliament, and votes exchanged hands on the open market like any other commodity – they cost £5 each at the turn of the eighteenth century in Honiton. Each town and village in the county had varying traditions and customs. Weights and measures, for example, were not uniform throughout the country, and the Devon farmer's wife sold her butter at 18 ounces per pound, whilst the Winchester bushel was widely recognized but not always used.

If the overcrowded houses and tenements of most towns were unpleasant, life was made no easier by the heavy taxes raised on many goods and transactions to finance the wars. The window tax, horse tax and a tax on servants each had an immediate effect on daily life. Some taxes were of a relatively transitory nature, like the tax on horses, which induced a man from Torbryan to ride a cow to market, whilst the blind windows still found in many houses are a more permanent reminder of the window tax.

Farms, houses, factories and churches are good permanent memorials to any age. In Devon, as elsewhere, they were built of local materials often in the latest style. The Georgian terraces of Exeter used pinkish-red bricks made locally, whilst local stone or cob was as popular as brick for new farmhouses. Each area had its distinctive materials which had been used harmoniously for centuries. The age of elegance was ushered in by the Georgian terraces, and the classical designs incorporated by Regency and early-Victorian buildings still give dignity to many places in Devon.

It was not until 1832 that the Political Reform Act reorganized national representation in Parliament, but even after this the Church and lords of the manor held sway. They were, however, caught up in the changes, particularly those in farming practice. The countryside of open fields and moorland was tamed with enclosures which allowed selective breeding of cattle, and the renewal and renovation of old buildings. Marshes were reclaimed and timber cut down, although it is only in the past ten years that one of the finest trees in the countryside has been decimated by Dutch Elm disease, and the visual quality of large parts of the county entirely lost.

Payne's pictures are of an idyllic countryside where the beauties of the county, its shipping and new buildings are placed in focus. He returned to Devon amongst the first of the tourists and artists who came in ever increasing numbers to enjoy and record its attraction. Much of the charm he depicted is recognizable today, although much has been lost. The pictures are an exceptional record of the county at a time of national change and are even more interesting when viewed against the local events and new life-styles that resulted in Devon's towns and villages.

During the early years of the nineteenth century William Payne developed and practised his talents and became well known for the creation and use of a bluish-grey colour, Payne's Grey. His contemporaries Sir Joshua Reynolds, from Plympton, Turner and Constable are infinitely better known today, although at the turn of the eighteenth century he would have lived comfortably in their company. It is thought that he was born between 1755 and 1760 and died in 1830 – the year when he last exhibited. In spite of the social unrest in the nation and poverty severe enough to cause bread riots, there was still a comfortable living to be had as a successful artist, and William Payne, having moved to London in 1790, built up a large and thriving teaching practice. At one point he was possibly the most sought after art master in London, but he outlived his fame and died in comparative obscurity.

Many of his paintings are of Devonshire scenes, and 87 of his original works are kept by the County Library Service. In order to make these scenes of an earlier Devon familiar to as many people as possible, the Amenities and Countryside Committee of Devon County Council have made Payne's pictures available for publication. Although he exhibited paintings between 1776 and 1830, those included in this book were painted between 1790 and 1800. There may be some artistic licence with details but they provide a romantic impression of Devon a little less than 200 years ago. They show beauty and the activities that created Devon's wealth and sustained its 343 000 inhabitants, three-quarters of which, including those resident in Exeter and Barnstaple, lived on the coast or on an estuary.

The paintings reproduced in this book are all approximately 5 inches by 6½

inches – a similar size to a modern postcard. Payne wrote titles underneath the paintings and these have been used as the captions printed here, complete with his sometimes eccentric spelling. Payne's painting techniques are simple, generally resulting in a dark foreground contrasting with lighter subject-matter and fine clouds scudding across the sky. His larger works held by galleries elsewhere are not so animated as the smaller ones, which are masterpieces of impressionism. Without clearly defining detail, Payne produced in economic fashion paintings that seem detailed.

Most of the paintings which he completed during the last ten years of the eighteenth century concern Devon's coast and estuaries as much as its countryside. The lively record of daily life shows that the scale of building, fishing and farming was still largely regulated by what men could achieve by their own physical endeavours and subject to the natural elements. It was not only a pictorial record of fact but also a prelude to the romantic Regency and early-Victorian period when the classical traditions were fashionable.

Payne seems to have spent the earlier part of his life in Plymouth, although this is uncertain. He certainly worked at Plymouth Dock as a civil engineer, and in 1780 probably held the office of Second Assistant to the Master Shipwright. His first exhibit for the Society of Artists of Great Britain was entitled 'A Landscape', and displayed in 1776 from an address in Park Street, Grosvenor Square. He exhibited between 1786 and 1789 giving Dock, Plymouth as an alternative to various London addresses. From 1790 he may have had a more permanent address in London at Thornhaugh Street, Bedford Square, but at some time before 1809 he moved to 10 North Crescent, Bedford Square. From 1810 until 1827 he exhibited material from his home in Upper Baker Street. Of the 108 pictures listed in his exhibition material, exactly half were of Devonshire scenes, whilst the other half included a variety mainly from Wales and Cornwall. This suggests that throughout his life he visited the haunts of his youth.

He was apparently encouraged by Sir Joshua Reynolds, who admired Payne's painting of the Cann slate quarries outside Plymouth. Reynolds, who had been brought up at Plympton and became Mayor of Plymouth, is believed to have helped several Devonian painters seeking fame and fortune. From 1790 it is likely that William Payne was working hard to become pre-eminent as a teacher and he was sufficiently successful for William Pyne (1769–1843) to write in the *Somerset House Gazette*:

That the method of instruction in the art of drawing landscape compositions, had never been reduced so completely to the degenerate notions of bad taste, as by this ingenious artist.

Mr Payne's drawings were regarded as striking novelties in style. His subjects in small, were brilliant in effect and executed with spirit – they were no sooner seen than admired, and almost every family of fashion were anxious that their sons and daughters should have the benefit of his tuition. Hence for a long period, in the noble mansions of St James Square and

Plymouth from Stonehouse Hill

Grosvenor Square and York Place, and Grosvenor Place, might be seen elegant groups of youthful amateurs manufacturing landscape, à la Payne.

Like most artists of his day, Payne travelled to well known places of beauty or interest, and was amongst the first tourists, or explorers of Devon. He probably returned from London to spend holidays in the county during which he completed his paintings. It is quite likely that he had relatives in Devon who were able to support him. In 1850 the Revd W. R. Payne was chaplain at the episcopal chapel of the Royal Naval Hospital, and others of the same name are recorded in Stonehouse as well a John Payne living in Princess Street, Devonport at that time.

It has recently been discovered that the paintings reproduced here previously belonged to the diarist the Revd John Swete, who travelled widely in Devon in the late eighteenth century and was himself an amateur painter. It seems likely that Payne accompanied him on some of these journeys, especially as Swete's watercolours attempt to follow Payne's style.

Because Payne's paintings dwelt on ships and water, often as foils to a particular landscape or feature, it is likely that he chose to avoid roads and pass along the coast or up estuaries. It has been appropriate to tread the same path, following the coast and considering Dartmoor and its newly discovered tourist attractions separately. In spite of the country's world-wide mercantile trade, until about 1820 people hesitated to face the perils of a trip along the miry ways of Britain. By this date the new turnpike roads had changed this reluctance to travel and brought many more people to live in or visit Devon.

The whole organization of society at the turn of the eighteenth century was affected by the lack of communication. Exeter, Taunton and Dorchester were the hubs of their counties to which gentlemen content to live on their country estates went for their entertainment and business. Sometimes they had a town house, and invariably if they were able to live in it without inconvenience they did so. Those with influence looked to the county town as a provincial capital, and to other towns as important for local events.

Similarly, ordinary people looked to their village or town as the centre of work, and life generally. It was through the manorial courts and the lord of the manor, or possibly by a local Justice of the Peace, that new and customary laws were maintained. The Church, with a well educated clergyman, often provided, together with the lord of the manor, a fund of wisdom and advice as well as some patronage. The poorer folk often lived restricted lives, unambitious and humdrum in a world lit by candles where superstition was just beginning to lose ground to scientific progress.

In retrospect, the general change in society is evident and pivots around the last decade of the eighteenth century and the first two of the nineteenth century. The particular developments recorded in different communities at different times build up the picture of change, whilst Payne's paintings capture the delights of the county at the start of it.

The Port of Plymouth

William Payne's familiarity with and love for the sea, shown in his pictures, came from living in or near Plymouth in his youth and from his employment in the dockyards. The Port of Plymouth extended to all the harbours, rivers and creeks between Looe on the west and the River Yealm in the east. It was often the centre of tragedies and successes arising from naval action during the war against France. For some there were considerable profits to be made, whilst some who left the newly built barracks in Stonehouse never returned. Others were wounded and on their return probably languished in the Royal Military Hospital, which had been built in 1797, before being discharged on a pittance.

The restrictions on shipping encouraged local merchants to act as agents for wealthy businessmen in London, Liverpool or Bristol, purchasing and transporting, under their direction, the vast quantities of prize goods sold in Plymouth. Although convoys of merchant ships were escorted through the dangerous seas, it was mainly increased coastal trade that gave the merchants of both Exeter and Plymouth their profit. Whilst the local merchants made money from the valuable prizes that came to Plymouth, the fighting men who had hoped for a share in the spoils could be less fortunate since their value was often appropriated by the Admiralty. The cost of a case in the prize courts of the Admiralty could equal any award made to the discontented sailors, and trouble-makers could find promotion harder to come by. When a ship did receive an award of prize money, its traditional distribution favoured the admiral who gave the order for the action rather more than the officers and crew who carried it out. This was one of the irritating aspects of unfair practice and corruption that permeated the Navy.

Marine Barracks nr Stonehouse

Mannadon nr Plymouth

A Commission of Naval Enquiry found that up to a quarter of the naval budget disappeared in a fraudulent manner during the war.

The population of Plymouth, Stonehouse and Dock (which was incorporated in 1824 to become the separate borough of Devonport, and thereby rival of the neighbouring borough of Plymouth) was only 43 000 in 1800, and not surprisingly, each of these small towns was dominated by the nearby hills and the expanse of Plymouth Sound. Today these old centres have grown and coalesced to become the single City of Plymouth, which was given this status only in 1918. It has sprawled and grown to house over 244 000, providing a variety of work but still maintaining its traditional connection with the Navy. It is more than twice the size of Exeter, as was the population of the three towns compared with that of the county town in 1800.

Plymouth was the most easterly of the three towns and Plymouth Dock furthest west, with Stonehouse, which seems to have had a higher social standing, between them. On three sides they were skirted and indented by the broad, deep and extensive creeks and harbours formed from the Tamar and Plym, which come together as Plymouth Sound. The harbours are still known as the Cattewater, Sutton Pool, Millbay, Stonehouse Pool and Hamoaze. During the Napoleonic Wars the extensive naval arsenal centred on the Hamoaze at Plymouth Dock was enlarged and the fortifications strengthened. Drake's Island in the Sound itself had for centuries been used for the defence of Plymouth and the barracks for 140 soldiers and 40 guns were ready to thwart any French invasion.

At the end of the eighteenth century Plymouth was a place of rumours and fears. There were good reasons for suspicion of spies and saboteurs. One of the best-known spies who tried to help the French to invade was Count Parades. He may have been the son of a Spanish count although his obscure claims to a title encouraged the suggestion that he was the son of a pastry-cook. He was certainly a good linguist and was supported by the French to come to England to find out about the disposition of troops, etc.

In Plymouth he got into the Citadel by bribing a sergeant and drew the defences. Similarly, by bribing people working at Dock he obtained details of its military layout. He returned to France and provided this useful information to de Satine, the French Minister, and illustrated how very poorly Plymouth was defended. It seemed unlikely that Plymouth could be so badly defended and Parades was not believed, so he returned with an emissary called Bertois to substantiate the truth.

When they arrived in Plymouth they were arrested but managed to escape by bribing their captors with £1500. Eventually they returned to France and suggested that an expedition of 4000 troops might be sent to Plymouth whilst rumours were spread that the ships were sailing from Brest to America. Instead of relying on surprise it was decided to send 30 000 French and Spanish troops in 66 ships. In August 1779 they anchored in Cawsand Bay and only the French admiral's timidity and belief that Plymouth was better prepared than it was stopped the invasion.

It was expected that the French would burn the docks. With little hope, and great activity, old cannon were dragged to defensive spots and a boom placed across the Cattewater. If the French did invade there was a danger that the prisoners would get loose and help, so they were marched out of the city to Exeter.

On 21 August a storm forced the French and Spanish out of the bay and Admiral Sir Charles Hardy, cruising with his fleet, sighted them leaving the vicinity of the Sound and gave chase. Both he and the French admiral took up battle stations but before a shot could be fired the French broke off contact and returned to Brest. The fears that this encounter created were enflamed by further scares in 1803 and 1805, when considerable efforts were made to provide defences for the town and dock.

Over several centuries Plymouth had grown up as a port and market-town in a congested and haphazard fashion with jumbled medieval buildings. In 1800 it was an insanitary and primitive borough which had the privilege, equal to that of nearby Plympton St Maurice, with a population of less than 2000, of sending two representatives to Parliament. Only after the end of the war was the borough improved by the removal of slums and the building of new

Pomlet Mills, Catwater

property in the latest elegant fashion. The increased wartime prosperity encouraged the Corporation to provide in 1809 a new market-place that covered three acres of ground off Cornwall Street, East Street and Drake Street, for the sale of meat, corn, fish, poultry, vegetables and displays of manufactured goods.

The manufacture of soap, sail-cloth, Roman cement, rope and twine were amongst the most important occupations and reflect Plymouth's mercantile trade. There were various mills, including one for flax, and a rope and cordage works. As in other Devon ports including Exeter, Teignmouth, Dartmouth, Brixham, Bideford and Barnstaple, busy shipbuilding yards satisfied wartime needs. Plymouth also had several iron foundries, breweries, steam sawing mills, a sugar refinery, starch works, and its own pottery.

The seeds of nineteenth-century improvement had begun to germinate early and there was already a public library with a large news-room in a handsome building constructed in Cornwall Street in 1811/12. The Plymouth Institution was another cultural innovation of the time, established in 1812 for the promotion of science, literature and the fine arts. Exhibitions of paintings were held here, including works by Devonshire artists. Amongst the most eminent were Northcote, Prout, Haydon, Ball and Bath, but Payne is not mentioned. The new Guildhall built in 1800 to replace the earlier one of 1606 soon became inadequate, although it contained a hall of justice and corporation offices as well as a police station and cells. A public dispensary was built in Catherine Street in 1808/9 for the benefit of the poor. The completion in 1813 of the theatre and hotel designed by Foulston set an example of elegance which was followed over the next fifty years to produce a city as attractive as spa towns like Cheltenham and Bath.

However chaotic, crowded and insanitary Plymouth's streets might have been in 1800, the Hoe provided a fine open space adjacent to the Citadel and overlooking the Sound for Plymothians to enjoy and where they could watch soldiers from the Citadel drilling. It must have provided an excellent vantage point for the naval review and sham naval fight staged for the benefit of George III and Queen Charlotte in 1789 when they visited Saltram. In 1799 there were mutinies in the Navy at Spithead, the Nore and Plymouth which were eventually quelled. Shortly after the execution of the ringleaders in Plymouth, a further plot by some marines at this tense time was discovered and the three ringleaders were sentenced to be shot. They were marched to the Hoe under a large military escort and, each kneeling on his own coffin, were executed by a firing squad before a large crowd of onlookers. Similarly, in 1815 the Hoe was crowded with thousands who visited Plymouth wishing to catch a glimpse of Napoleon on board the *Bellerophon*, which came to the port for eight days before he was taken aboard the *Northumberland* and transported into exile on St Helena.

At the time of the wars the Hoe was probably a fairly informal area. Only with their end was it improved with formal carriage-drives and public walks, helping to relieve the inevitable unemployment.

On the Cornish side, to the west of the harbour, the Sound was dominated by Mount Edgcumbe. From here during the war years the bustle of commerce, industry and warlike preparations could be seen, looking both up the Sound to Stonehouse and Plymouth Dock and down to the anchorage at Oreston and the Plym. The ancient mansion which stood on the promontory was destroyed in an air raid in 1941. It has since been rebuilt, and its grounds, run as a country park, are open to the public. In 1800, its gardens contained myrtles, cedars and a large number of flowering shrubs, with mature beeches, oaks, planes and other large trees adding attraction. The grounds are still well treed and gradually the gardens are being restored to their earlier beauty.

In 1794 the Admiralty ruled that midshipmen should be at least eleven years old before being appointed, and in a period when it was usual to be at work by fourteen or before, schooling was left largely to charities and the Corporation, and supplemented by dame-schools. Plymouth Grammar School was supported by the Corporation, but the increased population led to the founding of the Plymouth free schools in 1810. They provided for 400 boys and 200 girls and were run by the Church of England. They must have been sorely needed. National schools were opened in 1835 in Plymouth, although earlier (in 1809) at Dock, where rapid growth encouraged swifter action.

Mount Edgcumbe

Plymouth Sound from Stonehouse Hill

Stonehouse

Throughout the three towns various almshouses and workhouses provided for the old, poor and needy. Trusts and charities also helped those in need. Many were administered and supported by the Church of England, others were run by the Corporation, and however inadequate and haphazard it was, provision was made. It was a harsh age, made more so by the lack of organization and by traditions of independence and self-help, rather than because of any overall lack of humanitarian feelings. Sometimes, however, there were celebrations and feasting like the dinner given for the poor in 1819 on the proclamation of George IV. The rejoicings were even greater the next year, when the coronation took place, and 5000 were entertained in style in the market-place.

Payne's picture of Plymouth Sound from Stonehouse Hill is less detailed than much of his work and is rather tranquil and rural, but a particularly attractive painting entitled 'Stonehouse' gives a splendid impression of the bustle associated with the towns at this crucial time. Stonehouse Bridge, built in 1773, with the developing town beyond and a fine sailing-ship in the middle distance, provides a grandeur and quality not always too evident in some of his other pictures. The four labourers loading stone or slate on to a large wheeled cart with the horses patiently waiting give a welcome feeling of activity, whilst the old ferry-house beyond provides the kind of atmosphere that Capability Brown introduced into his landscapes by building decrepit hovels.

Stonehouse had a population of about 3000 in 1800 with Durnford Street its main thoroughfare. Recently Durnford Street with its Georgian houses has been improved and refurbished after some years of neglect. It is not dissimilar now to when it was first built for and admired by naval and military officers who wanted to live here. Within the town were several barracks capable of housing up to 3000 men, one of the most important being the Royal Marine Barracks for 700 completed in 1783. The development of the barracks for the Plymouth Division of the Royal Marines fostered the town's growth. Indeed, the popularity of the area was such that the chapel nearby, rebuilt in 1787, soon became too small.

The Royal Naval Hospital and Marine Barracks at Stonehouse were new when Payne painted them. The Hospital was painted from the Tavistock road, which appears to have been little more than a meandering unmade country lane, edged by high stone cliffs and unkempt verges suitable for grazing as well as allowing the occasional covered wagons to pass. The hospital buildings, constructed of stone with classical simplicity around a square in 1762, covered about 24 acres. They could accommodate 1200 patients, which as the war gathered pace after 1800, allowed 48850 wounded to be treated here over the next fourteen years. The Hospital was used through both the First and the Second World War but it has recently been demolished.

Stonehouse grew up at the same time as Dock (more generally known as Plymouth Dock) and in 1832 it was added by the Parliamentary Reform Act to the Borough of Devonport, as Dock had become. Of the three towns, Dock

Naval Hospital from the Tavistock Road

grew most quickly, from 3360 inhabitants in 1730 to 23750 in 1800, largely to house shipbuilders. The peace of 1802/3 probably checked the growth of all three towns but affected Dock the most. During this short period when the naval blockades were raised, Napoleon replenished his own dockyards, whilst Britain discharged half the Army and all volunteers, and broke up the Grand Fleet that had been stationed in Torbay. The battleships of the line were reduced from over 100 to about 40, many officers were placed on half-pay and 40000 sailors were discharged. Many ships were laid up in Plymouth, some no doubt requiring the attentions of shipwrights, caulkers, joiners, smiths, sawyers, ropemakers, painters, riggers, sailmakers and labourers, many of whom were laid off until the war resumed and the work was hurriedly put in hand.

Dock was bounded to the east by Stonehouse Pool and Creek, to the north by Morice Town and to the west by the spacious harbour of Hamoaze. Originally officers and artisans came daily from Plymouth to the dockyard, but by 1728 the Government had acquired a long lease of land occupied by the dockyard which encouraged its growth together with nearby housing. In Dock there was the victualling office for the Navy, barracks for the garrison, war prisons and the Gun Wharf, which covered five acres and was protected by a high wall to keep secure the numerous muskets, pistols and cutlasses stored there.

Dock was strongly fortified in the reign of George II with walls twelve feet high and became the centre of both naval and military government in 1725. Before this, naval and military government had been centred on the Citadel in Plymouth, which was built of limestone and granite, with a deep ditch on the east, north and west sides and a smaller fort below on the shore. With 120 gun emplacements on the upper parapets it was a formidable place, guarding the entrance to the harbour. The heavy batteries at Mount Wise, south-east of the town, included eight twenty-four pounders and two mortars with two small batteries below. They were designed to protect the entrance to the harbour from the sea, and Government House and Admiral's House stood prominently here. Government House was the private residence and military offices of the lieutenant-governor of the garrison; Admiral's House similarly served the port admiral. Various parades and celebrations were held here. The summit of the hill was used as a semaphore station to signal to ships passing up and down the Channel.

The redoubt and blockhouse on Mount Pleasant further protected these extensive lines of fortifications within which stood barracks, Government House and Admiral's House. In about 1810 the Government started to remodel and strengthen these defences, but when the Duke of Wellington inspected them in 1816 he considered them to be useless as a means of defence and work was abandoned with consequent misery and unemployment. The cry to reduce expenditure with the coming of peace may have had something to do with the judgement. After a decade, in 1826, the Royal William Victualling Yard in Stonehouse, designed by Sir John Rennie, was started, being completed in 1835. It confirmed Plymouth as one of the country's most important naval establishments. The whole of this building and its imposing entrance arches remain, as does the Breakwater started in 1812 to protect the Sound from bad weather, but completed only around 1850, on the basis of the plans produced by Messrs Rennie and Whidbey.

The dockyard, which had started merely as a work place for officers and artisans living in Plymouth, occupied more than 50 acres at the end of the eighteenth century and here many warships were built or repaired. In 1780 the Revd John Swete was impressed by the disposition of the docks although he noted that they were smaller than those at Portsmouth. He was particularly impressed by the basins hewn from the slate rock and being lined with freestone steps to help workers building new or careening old ships. The new North Dock was completed in 1789 and adequate for building or repairing the largest man-of-war, having a length of 254 feet and maximum width of 97 feet. It had a depth of 27 feet 8 inches, and after being cut from the solid rock, was lined with Portland stone.

Whilst at the dockyard, Swete also saw the *Phoenix*, the Spanish Admiral's ship taken by Sir George Rodney in the Mediterranean. It was there to be copper sheathed and refitted in a fashion considered suitable for its new owners. Later, when dining at the Passage Inn, Swete watched the *Bienfaisant* and *Ramilles*, which had been blown together and damaged at anchor during a gale, being towed up to the dockyard for repair.

The feeling of bustle and action is well translated by Payne in a picture of Government House at Devonport which shows mainly ships and seafaring men.

Dock was built within the parish of Stoke Damerel, which included the villages of Morice Town, Stoke and Higher Stoke. From the high land in the north-east of the parish it was possible to enjoy a view of all three towns and the shipping on the Sound. These growing villages were in effect suburbs of Dock where good-class houses for retired officers or similar people like wealthy merchants were built, separated from Dock mainly by the fortifications. The parish church of Stoke Damerel was close to the Military Hospital and had been enlarged in 1750 by the building of a third aisle. Today it is well within the built-up area of Plymouth, but Payne was able to show it to advantage in open country with a fine view over to Mount Edgcumbe.

Government House nr Devonport

Stoke Church and Mount Edgecumbe

Crabtree nr Plymouth

Saltram

Plymouth and its suburbs like those at Stoke were ill-lit places and sometimes it was dangerous to be out alone at night, although there were the normal provisions for keeping the peace by the night-watch and constables of the town. Watchmen were stationed at different vantage points, and in Plymouth the constables that visited different posts each night were at other times stationed in the Guildhall and easily found if a burglary or fire were to be reported. Nevertheless violence was not unknown and murder, burglary and highway robbery took place. One instance led a man named Richards who murdered a Mrs Smith in the hollow way beneath Stoke Church, possibly that shown in Payne's view, to be hung in chains on a gibbet erected on a mud bank and washed by the tide. The gibbet and chains remained as a reminder of the penalty for such crimes for a number of years afterwards, and probably vied with the convict hulks moored in the Sound as objects of morbid interest.

The suburbs of modern Plymouth have swept away any vestige of the idyllic rural scene found by Payne at Crabtree, although the view of Saltram, which must have been executed from only a mile or so away, retains much of its charm. The major alterations that transformed Saltram from a Tudor manor-house to one of the finest eighteenth-century mansions in the country and the largest house in Devon were completed by about 1758. The Amphitheatre and small temple seen below the house at the edge of the Plym in Payne's painting may have been completed then as well. It was Lady Catherine Poulett, daughter of the First Earl Poulett, who was mainly responsible for the aggrandizement of the house and grounds, rather than her husband John Parker. Saltram Woods, which stretch for nearly a mile along the south bank of the Plym, were enlarged at this time, and are still a beautiful sight across the water as one enters Plymouth from Marsh Mills.

Today the casual visitor to Saltram, which is owned by the National Trust, can spend an hour being conducted around it and enjoy the different periods of development, especially the alterations and additions made by Robert Adam in the 1770s for the second John Parker, who inherited the property in 1768. This John Parker was a member of Parliament from 1762 to 1784, the year in which he was created Baron Borringdon. The final alterations to the house were completed in 1810 by Foulston. He was responsible for adding the Doric porch topped with stone balustrades, for enlarging the central windows above it and for adding the Morley coats of arms in the pediment.

The Second Lord Borringdon was a man of considerable technical ability, although perhaps not as successful in monetary terms, and built some outstanding works often at his own expense. He constructed the cast-iron Laira Bridge across the Plym to the design of James Rendel, provided an embankment for the river, and reclaimed what is now called Chelson Meadow. In the 1820s Chelson Meadow became a popular horse-racing venue, but more recently it has become a refuse tip, which will eventually be used for sports fields and recreation again. Lord Borringdon received a gold medal from the Royal Society of Arts in 1808 for his achievements, which also included the construction of dry docks at Turnchapel in Cattewater Harbour.

Amongst the outstanding pictures kept at Saltram are several by Sir Joshua Reynolds, who died in 1792 and was a good friend of John Parker. The opportunity to become a friend of the Parkers, which allowed him to enjoy pheasant shooting and the genteel company of Saltram for many years, arose when he attended the grammar-school at Plympton, where his father, the Revd Samuel Reynolds, was headmaster. In return for the benefit of friendship and country pursuits, he probably advised wisely on the purchase of paintings. At the height of his career, when he became President of the Royal Academy, Reynolds was earning £6000 per year, and investing much of it in paintings.

Had he seen it, Sir Joshua might well have liked Payne's painting of Plympton St Maurice. Until only twenty years ago, Plympton St Maurice retained much of the unspoilt qualities reproduced in this painting, when it was little more than a quiet market-town on the edge of Plymouth, with a history that local people adamantly claim is longer. The grey slate and stone buildings clustering around the castle mound with the remains of the ancient castle and the parish church of Plympton St Maurice are pictured on a sunny

Plympton

day. It was a scene familiar for many years and no doubt fondly remembered by Northcote, Haydon and Eastlake, all successful eighteenth-century artists who came from Plymouth.

James Northcote was the younger son of Samuel Northcote, a watchmaker whose wife dealt in haberdashery. He was born in Market Street, Plymouth in 1746, and in spite of a poor education, with considerable determination defied his father's wishes and walked to London in 1771 to become a painter. Here he was helped by Sir Joshua Reynolds, whom he had first met when he had been touring with Samuel Johnson in Plymouth in 1762. Northcote's success as a painter, academician and author were a little at odds with his humble origins and his initial apprenticeship as a watchmaker. Before going to London he had painted local scenes but continued to work in London, where he died in 1831. Benjamin Haydon (1786–1846) was the son of a printer and publisher. After attending Plympton school between 1798 and 1801, he left for London in 1804 with £20, and prospered there. Eastlake was born at Plymouth in 1793, schooled at Plympton, and worked with conscientious and painstaking ambition to achieve success. In 1815 he was amongst those who hovered around the *Bellerophon*, and sketched Napoleon as he posed and waved to the people who came to stare at the man with the power to distribute thrones and make princes. Eastlake drew a small full-length portrait of Napoleon and another of the deposed Emperor with other figures, life size, for which he received £1000. Before he died, like Joshua Reynolds he had become distinguished and the President of the Royal Academy.

None of these worthies could be expected to find much beauty in the sprawling developments that have recently covered the areas between the old settlements of Plympton St Mary, the Ridgeway, Plympton St Maurice, Underwood, Plymstock, Goosewell, Hooe, Staddiscombe and Staddon, which in 1810 were all small hamlets or villages. At Oreston in the early nineteenth century, the quarrying of limestone for construction work like building the Breakwater helped to increase the numbers living and working there. Along the shores of the Cattewater and elsewhere were limekilns which further increased trade from Plymouth. At Turnchapel's new wet dock two frigates of 74 guns were built and launched: first the *Armada* in 1810, followed shortly after by the *Clarence*. As in other small settlements the war spurred growth.

Belle Vue nr Hooe

Radford House – Mr Harris

Nuncham Mills nr Boringdon

Nearby Borringdon seems to have kept its quiet rural charm, as Payne's painting of the Nuncham Mills suggests. There were not only corn-mills in the neighbourhood but also paper-mills and grist-mills, but Nuncham Mills were probably corn-mills. Agriculture and other rural activities profited from the prosperity that the wars brought to Plymouth, and the value of land around the edge of the towns increased to the benefit of the owners.

Since the end of the Napoleonic Wars Plymouth has been redeveloped twice. The growth of the towns which had begun in wartime continued during the next thirty years and it became a place of Regency elegance. Some basic services like the water supply from Dartmoor via the Devonport Leat, which took the place of wells and water sold from barrels after 1792, and Drake's (or Plymouth) Leat were investments able to support the considerable growth of the towns. Destruction during the Second World War followed by redevelopment of many areas built in the nineteenth century has left only relics of this earlier development. The harbours and quays, changed sometimes to meet new demands, remain an attractive reminder of a distinguished past which adds a lustre to the heart of the city. On a sunny day with Mount Edgcumbe as a backcloth, the view from the Hoe is as pleasant as those recorded by Payne, but inevitably the sixfold increase of population has destroyed the homely market-town feeling kept by some other Devon towns.

Oreston

Weir on the Tamar

The Tamar and Tavy

In a county which has more than its fair share of beautiful river valleys and estuaries, the Tamar and Tavy Valleys are outstanding. The best way to enjoy the Tamar is to take a pleasure trip from Plymouth up to Morewhellham. Here the quays, which during the nineteenth century were the most important on the river for despatching copper ore and tin, have recently been renovated and are operated as a working museum through a trust set up by the Dartington Hall Trust. A magnificent overshot water-wheel powered machinery to crush the ore for extraction of manganese and this turns slowly in the centre of the site, surrounded by overhead rails bearing wooden trucks. Various stone outbuildings used for mining have been restored, and nearby are the few cottages that make up the community. In 1808 William Gilpin, Prebendary of Salisbury Cathedral, took a trip up the Tamar: 'Procuring therefore a good boat and four stout hands from the *Ocean* man of war, then lying in the Hamoaze, we set sail with a flowing tide.' He recorded that he went 22 miles above Plymouth to the weir south of Gunnislake, probably the weir painted by Payne.

Gilpin's description of this natural boundary between Cornwall and Devon would not be out of place today. The broad estuary which sheltered the ships of the Navy had banks which whilst low were by no means flat, and were generally cultivated. The beauty of the woods of Antony and the scene both above and below Saltash caught his attention. The rocks around Cotehele provided some outstanding scenery as did the wooded hills beneath, on which stood a noble 'limekiln-castle':

At Cotehele house we landed, which is entirely surrounded with wood and shut out from the river. If it were a little opened, it might both see and be seen to advantage. To the river it would particularly present a good object; as it stands on a bold knoll, and is built in the form of a castle. But it is a deserted mansion, and occupied only as a farmhouse. Here we refreshed ourselves with tea and larded our bread, after the fashion of the country with clouted cream.

Round this old mansion grew some noble trees; and amongst them the Spanish chestnut, full grown and spread out in large massy limbs....

We now sailed a considerable way up the Tamar, and, during the whole voyage, had been almost solely obliged to the Cornish shores for amusement. But the Devonshire Coast, as if only collecting its strength, burst out upon us at Calstock, in a grander display of lofty banks adorned with woods, and rocks, than any we had yet seen, and continued without interruption through the space of a league.

But it is impossible to describe scenes, which though strongly marked, have no peculiar features. In Nature these lofty banks are infinitely varied. The face of each rock is different; it is naked, or it is adorned; or, if adorned, its ornaments are of different kinds.

Today the Tamar is a haven from the frantic pace of urban living where amateur fishermen and yachtsmen in small boats from sailing clubs at Weir Quay or Cargreen can enjoy its peace. Like Gilpin, the modern traveller can watch the frigates and smaller vessels of the Royal Navy and the host of privately owned yachts and boats in Plymouth's modern marinas, but unlike him can hardly expect the Royal Navy to provide transport. The boat from the *Ocean* must have been a fortunate chance since the man-of-war was Lord Collingwood's flagship and during 1808 spent some time cruising off Toulon.

At this time the prison hulks anchored between Torpoint and Saltash were intolerably crowded with French and Spanish prisoners, whose treatment was as harsh as might have been expected at a time when the Navy kept order by floggings and executions whenever necessary. Between 1808 and 1813 there were three old British ships converted to prison ships, including the *Bienfaisant* seen by the Revd John Swete on his visit to Plymouth in 1800. Eight French or Spanish warships which had been captured and brought to Plymouth as prizes were also used. One of the four French ships to escape from the Battle of Trafalgar on 21 October 1805 was the *Formidable*, although it was captured a month later and renamed the *Brave*. From this hulk, Captain Edward Hawkins, R.N. endeavoured to bring order and discipline to all the prisoners held in the eleven prison ships or in Mill Prison, which had been created from the tidal mills at Millbay in 1695. Corruption, drunkenness, escape attempts, overcrowding and illness were common to them all, and within the customary limits of the day he dealt with the prisoners as fairly as possible.

Because of the pressures of housing more and more prisoners on these miserable overcrowded hulks, the proposal of Sir Thomas Tyrwhitt for building 'a commodious and secure residence for these unfortunate men on Dartmoor, where the small value of land and the abundance of stone made building cheap,' was accepted. The five rectangular buildings remain today, massively brooding in the moorland landscape, where the clammy cold of long autumns and driving winter snow suggest penance and discomfort rather than idyllic views. Life here was undoubtedly rugged for the prisoners, crowded into hammock-filled rooms, but probably less miserable than on the prison hulks.

There was a high stone wall and look-out towers around the prison, with sufficient space between the wall and prison buildings for the captives to be seen. Undoubtedly the same rackets were pursued by the contractors who supplied the prisoners with food and other necessities, but the ability to trade with countryfolk, who held a market in the prison, reduced the privations. Prisoners could receive prize money or gifts from home and even earn a little by selling things they had made, thus ensuring some comfort in an existence which still encouraged escape attempts. The prisoners also supplemented their wealth by forging money and 'laundering' it through the market.

Building the prison in this remote spot helped to bring some prosperity to a desolate area. Various buildings, including two public houses and several homes for those working in the prison, created a small community here. The contractor's bakery was built close by, and isolated hamlets benefited from the money from trade with the prison. This development started the modern incursion on to the heights of Dartmoor which is so fiercely resisted today.

Returning to the Tamar, Saltash was only a small village in 1800 but has now become a substantial suburb of Plymouth, firmly attached by Brunel's railway bridge in 1859 and a toll-bridge built in the 1960s. However close the connection with Saltash may appear to outsiders, many Cornishmen feel the only improvement to their county would be if the Tamar were to widen its stream and leave Cornwall to float clear. The view from Saltash has changed less than the village itself, with sweeping expanses of water almost a mile across at full tide towards the sea, whilst up river the high banks and promontories hide successive bays. Along the banks there are a series of quays which are often rather derelict but which were once used by ferries, like that at Saltash, and furnished with limekilns for the farmers' needs.

During the wars the price of land multiplied 2½ times as the Navy's demand for fresh produce increased. The warmth and shelter of the Tamar Valley make it a favoured spot for market gardening, and a rainfall approaching 50 inches each year ensures good crops. An earlier spring than to the east of Plymouth and generally warm weather in early summer meant that, at the end of the nineteenth century, market gardens growing strawberries and raspberries were able to supply the London market two weeks before competitors. At the beginning of the century, the valley was able to satisfy the increased demand for vegetables and fruit for both the Navy and the growing towns of Plymouth.

In the latter part of the century Calstock became the distribution centre for soft fruit, but 80 years before it was of no note in a valley where the prolific cherry trees were left to their own tangled growth. The cider from a local apple called the Duffin had its own flavour and was valued as much as the renowned cider made in the South Hams. Fertilizers around 1800 were rather more basic than later in the century, and in addition to lime brought to the quays, or produced at them from burning limestone, sea-sand was used. This was mixed with earth, with scrapings from the lanes, including all the leaves, farmyard manure and loose earth, and when possible with rotten dung. Like the limestone, sea-sand was landed at the quays and carried along the narrow lanes to the steep sides of the valley on horseback. Because of the slopes and broken terrain, carts were rarely used in either the Tamar or the Tavy Valley.

Just before the confluence of the Tamar and Tavy is Warleigh Point, which is now a nature reserve run by the Devon Trust for Nature Conservation, but at the turn of the eighteenth century had recently been planted with oak and other hardwoods. Payne's view of Warleigh House from the hill above catches the attractive surroundings, which have changed little. The house and some of the outbuildings have been converted to flats and the Radcliffe family, who had held it from 1741 and still lived there in 1815, have gone. The prediction by the Revd John Swete, who passed by in 1797, that with care and good planting Warleigh Point could become one of the finest places in the land has proved correct.

To the north of Warleigh Point, squeezed between the Tamar and Tavy, the Bere Peninsula extends north and west to Gunnislake on the Tamar and north

Warleigh nr Tamerton — Mr Radcliff

Maristow – Mr Heywood

and east to Tavistock on the Tavy. Because it is bypassed by the main roads, it has a remote feeling, and the tranquillity is disrupted only for the months of summer when some visitors and a good number of boat owners enjoy the waters of both rivers. It is likely that until the large-scale mining of tin and copper in the eighteenth and nineteenth centuries, the silver mines were by far the most important workings in the area. There were several mines from which lead and silver were extracted and during the nineteenth century they provided between 80 and 100 oz of silver per ton of rock mined. Silver had been mined from about 1290, and although the pace of working and degree of success varied, this continued up to 1880. Between 1600 and 1800, it seems likely that relatively little mining took place, but in 1784 Christopher Gullet of Tavistock worked the South Hooe Mine and retrieved 6500 oz within a year. By 1809 silver was coming from all the ancient mines which had been reopened, and steam power and improved engineering techniques extended their usefulness until 1835. The introduction of new methods of ventilation allowed further mining but only in 1843 did Norton Johnson of the Tamar Silver Lead Company start to mine beneath the Tamar.

There is little to be seen today of this rich mining activity which after 1815 contributed greatly to the wealth of the valley, although the smelting of various ores gave rise to smogs and fumes during its heyday, from the 1840s. At Weir Quay there was a smelting works as well as limekilns, which are still there. By 1809 flatter land on the peninsula was often repeatedly being used for growing cereals rather than market gardening, so that the soil was showing signs of exhaustion. After 1815 it took some while for the soil to be put back into good heart, but this was achieved by the rotation of crops, introducing turnips and using an improved plough for a deeper tilth. Later bones were imported, often from France, and improved milling techniques allowed them to be ground to dust and used effectively as fertilizer.

About 1100 people were living on the Bere Peninsula in 1800 and 3400 by 1850. This growth arose with the development of the silver mines, and there was a similar expansion from 1100 to 4350 at Calstock, further up the Tamar, where the copper mines brought prosperity. Bere Alston was a rotten borough until its abolition by the Reform Act in 1832. It returned two members to Parliament, elected by those who had land in the borough and had paid three pence acknowledgement to the lord of the manor. At the turn of the century this was the Earl of Mount Edgcumbe and he was able to vary the number of electors at will by granting burgage-tenures to those whose support he needed. After the election it was customary to surrender the tenures. Today the village has grown still further with bungalows and modern houses around the older part. Several of the old Victorian terraced houses are slate hung and some are colour washed. Most seem to have been built when mining flourished.

Bere Ferrers, which in later Victorian times was renowned for strawberries, currants and gooseberries, which were grown in great quantities, sits on the edge of the Tavy. It is much smaller and more attractive than Bere Alston, which is in the centre of the peninsula. The oldest buildings in Bere Ferrers are the stone and slate cottages that line the narrow road down to the slipway. Here two or three houses and a village post office have a superb view over the Tavy to Blaxton Woods, and when the tide is out whimbrels, seagulls and curlews explore the mudflats, on which blue and white boats are moored. Nearby is St Andrew's, a pleasant and interesting fourteenth-century church. The road crosses marshland on a grey stone bridge with the Bible Christian Chapel, built in 1865, at the far end. It is possible to follow this road for a mile or so with glimpses of the Tavy already hemmed by steep hills, pastures and woodland. Sheep or red Devon cattle graze on the rich grassland, and on the opposite bank Maristow and its church are impressive.

Payne's picture shows a sailing vessel in the foreground, with 'WP 1793' conveniently signed on its sail, and the manor-house at Maristow in the distance. This fine building was gutted by fire two or three years ago but has now been converted to flats, keeping the pedimented Georgian façade. The estate once belonged to the Slannings and eventually through the Heywoods was left to four coheirs, the daughters of James Heywood, in 1798. It was then sold to Sir Masseh Lopes with the manors of Buckland, Walkhampton, Bickleigh and Shaugh Prior, and has remained in the Lopes estate of Lord Roborough ever since.

On the Tamar beyond Weir Quay, the broad rolling hills draw in and there are steeper sides to the valley. Opposite Weir Quay was Cargreen Quay, which eventually became disused after the First World War but had once been the medieval centre for cured Tamar salmon. Fishermen still cast their nets into the Tamar to catch salmon, and at Tavistock it is possible to see the fish fighting their way up towards Dartmoor from Abbey Bridge. Halton Quay, on the Tamar, was used for market-garden produce as well as despatching lead and silver but was closed in 1926. Further north is Cotehele Quay, below the largely Tudor manor-house built during the reign of Henry VII, which is now maintained, together with the attractive woodland surrounding it, by the National Trust.

The mineral resources of the Tamar and the effect of smelting, transportation and housing the miners were particularly evident around Calstock, Gunnislake and Morewhellham, where the meandering Tamar narrows but where it was still large enough for ships of up to 200 tons. The area served by the rivers included the triangle from Gunnislake north-east to Tavistock, ten miles away, and south to Weston Mill and Pennycross, now in the northern suburbs of Plymouth. The sublime view of the bridge at Weston Mill is lost for ever and there is no hint of the serene beauty that Payne enjoyed.

Thirty-thousand tons of copper were produced in this area in the first ten years of the nineteenth century. The swiftest and cheapest way for the ore to reach the market was by pack-horses to the quays of the Tamar, where it was either smelted or sent elsewhere by ship. In 1803 the Tavistock Canal Company started work to join Tavistock to the Tamar with a canal cut

Western Mills between Plymouth & Saltash

Pennycross Chapel

beneath Morwell Down to Morewhellham Quay. After fourteen accident-free years, it was finished and emerged 250 feet above the quay. An inclined plane allowed trollies to connect the canal with the quay, where during the middle years of the century many sailing ships moored and took on copper ore.

In 1811 seven copper mines were being worked in the Tamar and Tavy Valleys, producing 3500 tons of copper each year, but by 1850 the Devon Great Consols Mine near Tavistock, opened in 1845, was yielding about 1350 tons each month. Miners, earning between 13 and 15 shillings each week, lived in Tavistock and Gunnislake. In both places some early company houses were built by well-meaning employers: at Gunnislake John Williams provided cottages with sufficient gardens to keep a pig, whilst at Tavistock the solid stone and slate rows of workers' houses put up by the Duke of Bedford can still be seen from the Plymouth road.

Tavistock, even in 1815, was a market-town enjoying the wealth of copper and tin. In medieval times it was owned, together with the land around, by the Church. With the Reformation and disposal of the abbey lands in 1539/40 to Lord John Russell, an ancestor of the Bedfords, it became a secular town and enjoyed an equally long period of slow rural change, until the exploitation of minerals at the beginning of the nineteenth century. With the massive boom from copper mining just before 1850, the Duke of Bedford rebuilt the decaying centre of Tavistock in a dignified and imposing way using the greenish Hurdwick stone quarried nearby. The market buildings and Guildhall stand impressively in the centre making, together with the Church of St Eustachius, nearby early-Victorian or Regency properties and the Bedford Hotel, one of the most attractive centres for a market-town in the country.

There were already signs of change when the slate-hung houses and stone warehouse buildings by the canal and quays at Tavistock were built. A new library with 4000 books opened in 1799, while in 1822 the Duke of Bedford built the British School, for about 300 children, and in 1837 rebuilt the grammar-school. There were, of course, charitable trusts and institutions, and as a sign of the times the Tavistock Savings Bank opened in 1816. The Bedfords continued to take a benevolent interest in the running of the town during the period of growth that lasted until the latter part of the century. The population was 3420 in 1801, growing rapidly to 4720 in 1811 and to about 8000 by the middle of the century but falling to 5840 in 1900. Since then, Tavistock has been predominantly a market-town which has kept its interest and dignity without being spoiled by too much modern development. Recently Georgian property in Market Street below the railway viaduct has been restored by the Devon Historic Buildings Trust.

The Tavy brings clear waters from its source at Willsworthy on Dartmoor through the town. Downstream, it winds along serpentine channels below steep well-wooded hillsides to Drake's Weir and Denham Bridge beyond. Whilst the detail may be changed, the spirit of this remote and beautiful place has been unaltered for two centuries.

Sir Francis Drake's Weir, Tavey

At the edge of Gunnislake the road from Tavistock passes over New Bridge, an imposing old stone bridge with room for a single line of cars and refuges for pedestrians. A small white toll-house on the Devon side heralds magnificent views along the well-wooded valley of the Tamar, flowing a long way below. Less attractive is the sight of Gunnislake, which sprawls over the hillside as it has done since its early growth at the end of the eighteenth century. There are a good number of modern houses and bungalows and some Victorian terraced cottages. Odd relics of the mining past remain and the development of Calstock and Gunnislake during the mining boom has left quays at Calstock which shipped tin from nearby Kit Hill and Drakewalls starting before the Napoleonic Wars. The Gunnislake Old Mine produced copper in the latter part of the eighteenth century and continued most successfully in the war period. Growth of the settlements also depended on paper making, manufacture of coarse earthenware and quarrying granite from Kit Hill and Gunnislake. Some granite was used in the fortifications and dockyards of Plymouth and some exported to London and elsewhere for kerbstones or buildings, including Blackfriars Bridge.

Denham Bridge, Tavey

The granite quarries opened by Pearson in 1808 at Gunnislake lasted for a century and were one of the largest employers in the area. At nearby Hingston Down granite for roadstone was quarried, and there are still quarries for roadstone in the area. In 1794 it was proposed to construct a canal using navigable parts of the Tamar to transport goods as far as North Tamerton Bridge, 30 miles from Morewhellham. It was mainly intended for lime, but eventually only about 3 miles between Morewhellham Quay and Weirhead were built in 1808.

It was, however, between 1840 and 1860 that exploitation of all the minerals found in the Tamar and Tavy Valleys was at its peak and the valleys suffered pollution as well as enjoying prosperity. Fortunately landowners like the Duke of Bedford, the Duchy of Cornwall, the Edgcumbe and Cotehele estates were less enthusiastic about allowing chaotic mineral workings than they were about preserving the sylvan beauty of the area and its farming activities, no doubt partly for the good cover for pheasants thus provided.

Tin, copper, lead, silver, manganese, arsenic and fluor-spar were mined in considerable quantities, smelted and exported along the waters of the Tamar, but the valleys have returned with few scars to the state they were in when Gilpin saw them in 1808. The mudflats, so grey in winter light, are fine areas for water birds, widgeon, Brent geese, curlews, lapwings, herons and gulls. Today's industrial landscape is represented by the 400 kV pylons that cross both rivers and the impressive stone railway bridges, although the wires are the more intrusive. Whilst the scale of farming and its methods have changed, with fewer fruit growers and most of the cherry trees gone, the valley's beauty depends once more on farming. The shipbuilding that took place on a small scale after 1820 is no longer of importance. No longer do paddle steamers sail majestically up the Tamar, but in the tradition of those who first came to explore in the nineteenth century, tourists can still savour this attractive area from the river. Payne would feel more at home now than he would have done fifty years after he painted his idyllic river scenes.

The South Devon Coast and the Dart Estuary

The population and towns have grown markedly more in Devon than in most other places in the country but it is still possible to find unspoilt countryside and coast. Narrow winding roads and the intrusive waters of the Yealm, Erme, Avon, Kingsbridge and Dart estuaries create barriers that have helped to limit growth, so that this area has stayed attractively remote. Its tiny villages and small towns have grown with the normal accretions of bungalows and houses, but not excessively so in most cases. The coast between Dartmouth and Plymouth still has only about 25 000 inhabitants, of which 6000 live at Dartmouth, 4500 at Kingsbridge, 3000 at Wembury and 2500 at Salcombe. Although the pace and techniques have changed, farming and fishing still provide most jobs, directly or indirectly.

Overlooking the Yealm, the first estuary encountered east of Plymouth, in an imposing position, is Wembury House. It was built in 1803 by Thomas Lockyer of Plymouth to take the place of a much larger mansion. Nearby is the attractive village of Wembury, which grew from 1400 inhabitants in 1961 to 3300 twenty years later. All that was here in 1800 was a scattered settlement of fewer than 600 people dependent on farms or fishing. The outstanding natural beauty of the area was not lost on visitors who passed along the coast and saw the Great Mew Stone, Blackstone Rocks and Wembury Point. The Mew Stone, which rises menacingly at the river's entrance, leaves a sufficient channel for coastal craft to find a haven there.

There are a number of good houses in the area, including Kitley, built in 1825 in the Elizabethan style by Repton, and Puslinch, which has hardly altered since it was built by James Yonge about 1720. Puslinch looks across the Yealm Estuary not far from Yealmpton, a town which, like Wembury,

Wembury House — Lord Camden's

Puslinch nr Yealmpton

Fleet House – Mr Bulteel

houses a good number of Plymouth commuters. It is a marvellous spot with boats, rivers and enticing countryside. No wonder about a fifth of its population chose to retire here. The idyllic surroundings of St Bartholomew's Church have changed and houses have been built close by. The church was substantially reconstructed in Victorian times and incorporates local Kitley limestone, which has been attractively polished to a marble finish. The columns inside are grey unpolished limestone banded with black polished marble to good effect. The red stone font with a black base is outstanding, so too is the red marble screen. The arches and windows are of Caenstone and the walls decorated with biblical texts.

Fleet House at Brixton was substantially altered by Norman Shaw in 1878, although he kept the old west wing, which was part of the Elizabethan manor and which has two storeys with gables and retains the earlier decorative features. The house also incorporates other parts of the earlier building altered or completed in 1835. Its well-detailed Gothic façade and the views over the River Erme and the rolling, well-wooded countryside around show the care taken in siting an imposing home and maintaining a beautiful setting. It is approached by a long drive from the Brixton road through some fine

mature parkland planted with oak, sweet chestnut, horsechestnut and other deciduous trees and regularly opened to the public.

In the nineteenth century limestone was brought up the River Erme in barges and burnt in the kilns at its side. The entrance to the river is partly blocked by a spit of sand and gravel, and in 1795 after a great storm, another barrage of sand and gravel was thrown up and prevented shipping entering. Before any action could be taken to dig a channel and free the harbour another storm washed the obstruction away, leaving the harbour accessible again. In 1800 there were 1120 villagers living in the parish of Holbeton, which borders the Erme. Much of it was once owned by the Perring family, whose seat was Membland Hall, from which they enjoyed fine views of Bigbury Bay. In 1803 Sir John Perring became Lord Mayor of London and in 1808 was created a baron.

Not far inland, with a population of less than 2000 in 1800 and only double that now, is Modbury, one of the most attractive towns in Devon. Like Totnes and Dartmouth it has many ancient buildings whose fronts are slate hung, the common style of the South Hams. Modern development is tucked away behind the earlier main streets, which have kept the variety, texture and

Yalmton

colour of natural materials used in the early nineteenth century. Modbury's steep roads, raised pavements and the ancient houses that face on to them are delightful. Four main streets, all downward sloping, converge at the bottom of the hills on which the town is built. Modern traffic management has destroyed the ancient Red Cow public house close to the junction, but fortunately such acts of vandalism to support progress have been few. Modbury has prospered over the ages, particularly in Georgian times if the variety and number of Georgian doorways are evidence. Traine, an attractive property on the north side of the town, incorporates the grandeur associated with better-quality buildings, with a white painted stucco front and columns.

The old market-town atmosphere still permeates Modbury through splendid small shops and public houses which carry on past traditions. Personal attention for the shopper making daily visits for bread or meat in the unhurried fashion of earlier days can be consolidated with a good snack beneath ancient beams at the Exeter Inn. Slow growth has ensured rather greater preservation as a whole than elsewhere. During the early years of the nineteenth century three Nonconformist chapels were built and the conversion of an Independent chapel to a national school was completed. The town is an attractive museum of Georgian or Victorian buildings which contributes to the pleasure of modern living.

Payne only painted Brent (Mill) Bridge on the Avon, above the estuary, close to South Brent (see page 45). The estuary, a refuge for wildlife, can be navigated by small boats. In 1800, barges carrying limestone or other goods passed along it up to Aveton Gifford, which is close to the three-arch stone bridge that crosses the river rather more than three miles inland. Salmon were caught in the river and there was good fishing for those living in the scattered parish. Although there are sandy beaches at Challaborough and near South Milton, most of the coastline is inaccessible because of the impressive cliffs. There are spectacular views around Bolt Tail and inhabitants of the two small villages at Hope Cove, grown from the hamlets of 200 years ago, have enviable opportunities to enjoy them.

Between Bolt Tail and Bolt Head, the cliffs that rise from 50 to 400 feet and the rocks indenting the coastline are obviously a menace for sailors but a haven for wildlife. Salcombe is situated at the mouth of the estuary which runs up to Kingsbridge. These are the two southernmost towns in the county, with some of the mildest weather, so much so that at the turn of the eighteenth century Moult, a villa built in 1764, and Woodville, built in 1797, were each successfully growing orange, lemon and olive trees in the open. At that time Mr Yates of Woodville, renamed Woodcott, used his sheltered garden to grow an aloe which in 1820 was 27 feet tall and flowered prolifically.

Salcombe is pleasantly and picturesquely situated on the western side of the estuary, and in recent years the more-modern houses have spread up the hill away from the older streets by the harbour. It was well known for pilchards, which between the middle of July and the end of autumn would arrive in great numbers, although as with all fishing this could not be relied

on. In those hard times it was not surprising that fishing was supplemented by smuggling and taking whatever wrecks might offer. The Napoleonic Wars brought a bonus in these things because excise cutters were used for the war effort. If a vessel went aground the locals felt it was a lawful prize and rejoiced. On one occasion a grounded vessel was systematically plundered, but before much had been 'saved' a puff of wind took her off the beach and she was able to resume her course. There was no rejoicing but a volley of curses from disappointed plunderers.

This was not an isolated case, and the lack of generosity of impoverished people and the wartime needs prompted the introduction of the first lifeboat in Devon, at Plymouth, in 1803. In 1821 the Water Guard, who a year later became coastguards, with the duty to aid sailors and help save lives, were introduced along the coasts. Coastguard cottages and stations still stand, and the beats of the coastguards have often been combined with even older tracks to create the coastal paths.

Salcombe was also a good fishing ground for crabs and lobsters, as it still is: the Salcombe and Dartmouth crabbers, together with a smaller number from Hope Cove and Hallsands/Beesands, landed catches worth about £1.7 million in 1980. Looking across towards East Portlemouth from the slips at Salcombe, the sight of the anchored crabbers and the many smaller craft belonging to weekend sailors is reminiscent of mid-Victorian days, when the estuary was crowded with many more fishing vessels.

Salcombe Castle, built for the defence of the harbour, was put into good condition during the Civil War in the seventeenth century, but later allowed to decay and collapse until now there is relatively little left. As well as fish, culm, foreign fruit and groceries were landed at Salcombe, although many ships passed up the estuary to Kingsbridge. Shipbuilders plied their trade and in 1850 there were three shipbuilders' yards. During the early part of the century corn, flour, malt, potatoes and slate left the harbour.

Kingsbridge, which lies about six miles to the north of Salcombe at the head of the estuary, is a pleasant small town. The estuary has a number of creeks which create most attractive scenery where fishermen and farmers have over the ages quietly gone about their business. Like Modbury and Totnes, Kingsbridge is built on hillsides and the older parts have many slate-hung buildings. It has kept small shops along the road from the quay as it slowly curves uphill to the Town Hall with its interesting clock, built in 1875, and the King's Arms and old grammar-school beyond. A little more than half way up, by the Town Hall, is the Shambles, the old market-house, rebuilt in 1796 and carried over the pavement on granite columns, with St Edmund's, the parish church, behind it.

The quay is no longer used by the coastal vessels that brought coal and other general merchandise for most of the nineteenth century; instead smaller pleasure craft and wheeling sea-gulls create a seaside atmosphere. A modern sports centre has been built close by, out of scale and with materials that harshly conflict with the older buildings. When seen from the main street it has only its function to recommend it. In 1800 the prosperous farming community used Kingsbridge's market and woollen-mills, although the latter declined after 1815. Markets were held in the parish of Dodbrooke until the end of the eighteenth century, after which only those at Kingsbridge were maintained and enlarged by a large cattle market in 1773. In 1804 the town acquired a barracks at Dodbrooke for 600 men, but at the end of the war it was taken down except for the hospital and gun room.

Many of the delightful buildings seen as the main road gradually curves uphill are early Victorian although new and modernized premises had already been put up in 1800. There are similar interesting but more humble buildings in Dodbrooke, where raised pavements and stone terraced homes line the road to the quay. By the end of the Napoleonic Wars there was a Friends meeting-house, built about 1659, a Baptist chapel, rebuilt in 1799, and a Wesleyan chapel, built in 1815, as well as the thirteenth-century parish church, to satisfy the spiritual needs of the town.

During the nineteenth century fast Salcombe schooners suitable for transporting citrus fruit, etc., were built along the estuary. The prosperity midway through the century allowed owners and masters of these vessels to live comfortably and build substantial houses. Today, like other estuaries, it is a lively place with its share of blue-and-white sailing dinghies, motorboats and surfboarders.

Leaving the Kingsbridge Estuary and passing by the steep cliffs to Prawle and Start Point, the countryside seems remote. To the north, Hallsands, Beesands and Slapton Sands are particularly attractive to holiday-makers with children. The natural phenomenon of Slapton Ley, a freshwater lake of about 300 acres separated from the sea only by a relatively narrow ridge, has always attracted tourists like Payne. He evidently stopped nearby and painted the Ley as well as a beach scene near the northern end showing Stoke Fleming Church in the distance. The scene has changed little, although in the holiday season a good many enjoy good swimming there.

Slapton Sands & the Start Point

Stoke Fleming and Mr Trig's House from Slapton Sands

Torcross, at the southern end of the Ley, had only a single line of houses around 1800, lived in during the summer months by families from neighbouring towns. From time to time great shoals of mackerel appeared in the sea in the vicinity, so that people from Slapton and Stokenham were able to bring horses and donkeys to carry off full panniers of fish. Slapton is about a mile from the shore and set neatly amongst rolling hills with a pleasant stone church at its centre. An interesting feature is an 80 foot tower, all that remains of Poole Priory, which had been the seat of the Hawkings but had become dilapidated before 1800, when all but this landmark was removed. The village has grown since this time, but the old centre with whitewashed cottages with large chimney stacks and slate or thatched roofs keeps its charm. As a girl on a pony rides past it could be a film set for a Victorian pastoral scene. There are two good pubs including the Town Inn, claiming to date from 1347, when it was six workmen's cottages, and a Field Centre, whose students study the abundant fish and bird life of the Ley.

On the edge of the beach, at the centre of the Ley, there is a column to commemorate the preparation by American soldiers who took part in the D-Day landings in Normandy in June 1944. A whole stretch of coastline was evacuated and appropriated for use as a battle practice area. It included the villages of Blackawton, Chillington, East Allington, Slapton, Kenham, Strete and Torcross, together with many outlying farms. The memorial stands where the old Cellar Hotel was in 1800 before being demolished during the last war. One hundred and fifty years ago it was felt to be well fitted for the reception of guests. The nearby Manor House Hotel was burnt down some years ago, and recently its grounds have been made into an excellent picnic site. At the other end of the Ley, close to Torcross, a Sherman tank that had been lost at sea was restored in 1984 as a memorial to the Americans killed during the battle practice.

The beauty of the River Dart was well known to travellers at the end of the eighteenth century and Payne paid considerable attention to it. A picture of Dartmouth with its anchorage seems to have been drawn on the opposite side of the estuary near Kingswear, close to the ruins of an ancient castle. The present quays, which have recently been repaired, were not developed until the end of the nineteenth century. In their place was a foreshore of mud with the quays in use then west of today's line.

Dartmouth is a well sheltered harbour and the hills encircling it are still wooded and attractive. In Payne's day there was sufficient anchorage for up to 500 sailing vessels. Many of those using the harbour were engaged in the Newfoundland trade, which involved ships exporting manufactured goods or produce for the settlers, then sailing from the fisheries, which were particularly prolific with cod, to different ports of the Mediterranean, returning to England carrying wine, oil and fruit. Many of the merchants engaged in this trade built homes close to the Quay, and some of these enhance the town today. Two things damaged this trade during the Napoleonic Wars. First, trade was restricted by the danger from French

warships, although convoys were formed to protect merchant ships. At the same time, because of the disruption of trade the colonists developed their own shipbuilding and manufacturing, so that after the war they were no longer so dependent on English shipping or goods. In 1791, Dartmouth had 112 ships plying the Newfoundland trade. After the war there were about sixty, then there was a further gradual decline. The loss of this staple trade reduced the importance of Dartmouth.

Dartmouth's prosperity had been ensured by the success of the woollen trade, with cloth passing through from Totnes, and this also declined after the war. The importance of the town as a trading centre had gone by the middle of the nineteenth century, although its value as a market-town and fishery continued. For the first part of the century it was also a well-used harbour for ships trading along the coast. When Danniell visited it early in the 1820s he saw Torbay boats, distinguished by having tanned sails. These were tinged red in the process of tanning, which was expected to preserve them.

The imposing entrance to the harbour has a castle on either side. At one time it was possible to place a chain across the entrance to keep any enemy force out. In 1850 White recorded that Dartmouth Castle still had a governor, fort major and master gunner, and it probably had the same armaments of six twelve pounders and four eighteen pounders in 1815. At Bayards Cove is another fortified position built in 1509 with ten irregular gun ports. Within the past ten years the little quay nearby has been recobbled and fishermen leaving their lobster-pots on it add an appropriate work-a-day feel. The Customs House of 1734 that overlooks it and Morocco House next door, possibly the home of a trader or ship's captain who made his money in those parts, are part of an attractive Georgian terrace and group of earlier houses close to the fortifications.

There was a ferry from Kingswear in 1800 and now near Bayards Cove there is the lower ferry slip serving the town, operated by British Rail; the upper ferry slip is privately run. An attractive feature of Kingswear is the arrival of steam trains from Paignton, whose passengers are ferried across to Dartmouth. Even by Devon standards Dartmouth is a remarkably attractive town with some excellent buildings by its quays and boat float. Amongst the older pubs is the Cherubs, a free house on Horn Hill, which rises steeply as a footway of yellow brick paviours. It claims a date of 1380 and stands opposite a rather larger Tudor property. Nearby a new building for the Royal British Legion, together with the well-restored Palladium House, maintains the character of this small square near the church. The market square has kept some of its old buildings as well as the original paving around them, and an array of good early-Victorian buildings and the Methodist church, restored in 1938, form a pleasant shopping place. The town has parallel streets built along the hillsides with houses which look over one another to the harbour. The roads are connected by a series of steep steps built of stone or brick paviour. There is scarcely a property in the town which is not well maintained and, if rendered, colour washed in a pastel shade.

Dartmouth

Wotton — Sir F. Rogers

This light colouring might not have been considered so desirable in the early nineteenth century. At this time the prevailing colour was grey, from the abundance of slate roofs and slate-hung buildings. There was also a tradition of painting properties grey so that the whole town was 'uniformly, neatly and modestly grey'. At this time the twisting narrow streets were better recognized as belonging to three former villages, Clifton, Dartmouth and Hardness, which although they had come together as a single town kept their local loyalties.

The fishermen of Dartmouth concentrate on crabbing today but in the past, when fish were more numerous, they sometimes benefited from porpoises chasing shoals of pilchard into the harbour. If the fish were in sufficient numbers their leaping and flurries in the water attracted the attention of the townsfolk, then every boat that could float would put out to net them.

During the Napoleonic Wars fourteen frigates were built at Dartmouth and shipbuilding remained an important industry until late in the century. At Noss, just above the town, the yards are used for a marina, which is entirely appropriate for the tourists who support the harbour and without whom it would be a poorer place.

As in most towns of its size, there was considerable social activity, reflected particularly by the churches. The old church of St Petrox standing next to the fortifications at the entrance to the harbour is picturesque, but St Saviour's in the centre is equally interesting. It has some good carving including a screen of 1480 with sixteen panels decorated with pictures of saints. The screen's carving, with vine leaves and grapes, is not uncommon. The main door to the church has the year 1631 on it but may date from the late fourteenth century. It is strapped with iron decorations in the form of the tree of life, and two beasts forming the strap hinges which look enough like lions from a crusader's shield to warrant this assumption.

The Independent chapel, Wesleyan chapel and Baptist chapel had all been built before 1820 and the imposing size of the Methodist chapel, overlooking the market car-park, shows its importance at this time.

Only about 7500 people lived in the Dart Valley in the early part of the nineteenth century. About 18000 live within its well-wooded slopes, creeks and fertile land now but this has not affected the attraction of the river and surrounding countryside. Payne's progress up river past the home of Sir Walter Raleigh at Greenway shows it to be a broad expanse of water with a brig and smaller boats probably going up to Totnes. The road to Greenway, through an area of hardwoods and an avenue of beech, looks over the Dart to Dittisham as the river narrows from the wide lake-like expanse at Galmpton Creek. Continuing the service of centuries, a ferry runs during the summer months and Greenway is the centre for a good many pleasure craft. For a small sum one can cross the river to enjoy the beauty and hospitality of Dittisham, which has become a substantial village. It has several narrow roads and a number of ancient houses with a main street that passes down the hill to the Ferryboat Inn and buildings that line the waterside.

Stacks of lobster-pots at the Greenway slip and trees that sprout from the water's edge make an attractive picture. The painting of Waddeton, the house of Sir Frederick Rogers, which at the beginning of the nineteenth century was sold to Henry Studdy, shows a ferry and passengers with their horses about to embark, probably at Greenway. Today the hilly countryside around Watton or Waddeton Court is charming parkland, planted with a variety of deciduous and coniferous trees.

Stoke Gabriel had a population of only about 530 in 1800 and its ancient Church of St Peter stood above a small creek which had been dammed to turn the wheels of tidal corn-mills. In the church there is a fifteenth-century rood-screen with painted panels and carved pulpit, as well as a display of old documents about earlier parishioners. Under the Elizabethan Poor Laws each parish was expected to support its own poor. John Elliott was a shoemaker and in 1792 he was destitute in Dittisham, having come from Stoke Gabriel with his wife and nine-month-old child. Because there was no work for him he was sent back to Stoke in August 1792. Without

Greenway — Sir Walter Raleigh

Mills at Stoke on the River Dart

acceptable property qualifications people were restricted in their travelling from parish to parish, but the needs of society after the Napoleonic Wars saw an end to this. Today, with a much larger population, the village still keeps its beautiful wooded views of the river although the mills have gone and a boat slip extends into the Dart instead. Within the village the remains of what in 1800 were extensive cider orchards lean drunkenly, imparting a pleasant spaciousness. Near St Peter's along the cobbled way is the Church House Inn, a pleasant luncheon spot with moulded black beams and wooden plank and muntin partitions.

On the opposite bank to Stoke Gabriel, hidden within the hills, are Cornworthy and Ashprington, with Bow Creek and the hamlet of Tuckenhay between them. Cornworthy has its share of ancient stone farmhouses and cottages amongst the newer development. St Peter's Church has a delightfully lopsided porch which, like the vestry, was probably added in the sixteenth century. The church itself lies to the east of the village and dates mainly from the fourteenth century. Like the older buildings in the village, it was built of the local stone and is appropriately as simple inside as out.

Bow Creek stretches in to Tuckenhay, which is reached from Cornworthy along the well-named Corkscrew Hill. There were once two mills supporting this tiny community: a corn-mill and a paper-mill. Some of the mill buildings have been converted to other uses like flats or holiday homes, and the mill clock prominently displays the wrong time from its lofty tower. Along the southern bank of Bow Creek towards Cornworthy, the rotting ribs of ancient sailing vessels stick up from the mud as memorials to past trade. After crossing the humpbacked Bow Bridge and winding uphill one reaches Ashprington.

Above the village St David's Church is built of dunstone with red sandstone dressings. Its tower had a ring of five bells until 1975, when they were so unsafe that they had to be removed by helicopter, and since 1978 a single bell has been hung. Church Barn, close to the church, has kept the round stone pillars exposed in the front façade, while another equally good conversion of a barn using slate hanging and stone stands close to the war memorial. The village has grown in recent years, but on a summer's day with a farmer driving his sheep through the centre of the village past the war-memorial cross and the stone and slate houses, it feels as if there has been little change for a hundred years. It is an attractive spot and Sharpham Manor, built between 1776 and 1820, is surrounded by fine wooded parkland.

In spite of the narrow channels and limited depth, modern timber-ships carry loads up to Totnes just as they have done for centuries. During the nineteenth century the coal, timber and culm imports were balanced by the export of cider, farm produce and corn. After 1833 the Commissioners of the River Dart improved the navigation for ships of up to 150 tons. Today the Plains have some of the finest stone and slate warehouses that can be found in the county, in a state of decay but being renovated. These formidable four-storey buildings, when converted into shops and flats, will incorporate

Sharpham on the Dart

the ancient hopes, sweat and toil of the merchants of Totnes, on whose success the town has prospered.

Professor W. G. Hoskins asserted that Totnes was the most historically interesting town in Devon after Plymouth and Exeter. Certainly, passing up Fore Street and High Street to the top end of town, there are sufficient sixteenth- and seventeenth-century buildings to emphasize its early significance. Both wool and tin were important when it was one of the pre-eminent trading centres in the country. Its picturesque qualities are enhanced by the variety of buildings and there are few large shops to spoil the intimate nature of the streets, with modest wooden fascias and not too many garish advertisements.

The old town had four gates, and East Gate, spanning the main street half way up the hill and dividing High Street and Fore Street, is an attractive focal point. The variety and interest in Fore Street is created by the mingling of gables, slate hanging, pitched roofs, bay windows, stone buildings and stucco fronts. The continuous frontage is sometimes broken and a building set back from the road. The old King Edward VI grammar-school has sadly lost the ivy that festooned its brick façade, possibly because of the misguided comments of the late Alec Clifton Taylor in his excellent television programme about this enchanting town. North Gate, below the Norman castle with its immense round keep on top of a large artificial mound, is built of red sandstone and is imposingly whole. Some attractive cottages with entrances up steps at first-floor level curve round the side of the castle mound. West Gate, at the junction of High Street and South Street, south of the castle, and South Gate, close to the new market building, were demolished many years ago.

St Mary's Church, just above East Gate, was rebuilt using red stone in the fifteenth century and has a high tower at the west end. It contains a carved Beer stone pulpit and rood-screen which were added in 1459/60 by the Corporation. Opposite is Nicholas Ball's house with the year 1585 moulded into an ornate black-and-white plasterwork pattern. The quality of the exterior plaster is matched by an interior ceiling of strapwork moulding on the first floor. Like other houses in the town, as well as the Guildhall to the rear of the church, this building shows the plastering skills available in sixteenth-century Totnes. Beyond East Gate the vista is closed by the church and the end of the Butter Walk, which spans the pavement on granite columns, and which in 1800 would have sheltered the farmers' wives who sold their wares beneath.

Almost every house in High Street and Fore Street has a point of interest. So too have the lanes and alleys like Atherton Lane off Fore Street, with paviours edged with cobbles and colour-washed cottages gaily decorated with pots of flowers. The Ramparts Walk with cobblestones and stone walls starting at East Gate sweeps round to the slate-hung Guildhall. On the other side of High Street, South Street formed the edge of the oldest part of Totnes, and now contains an enjoyable variety of buildings and occupations. A great deal of red and grey stone used in the buildings and walls ensures cohesion that only older development achieves. Small alley-ways and yard doors provide speculative interest and a glimpse of a community that still lives in the heart of a town. Although it is likely that the quality of buildings and their fittings have been improved, builders have used the skills and heritage of the past with feeling. An outstanding case of this was the preservation of the magnificent cider warehouse called the Blue Ball, built around 1805 and converted in about 1973 to flats. The mellow reddish-brown stonework epitomizes the quality of earlier times and the more modern materials and residential use do not conflict with it.

It was recorded in 1850 that water was provided from springs at the top end of town and flowed down either side of the High Street. Although this has changed, Leechwell, close to the Kingsbridge Inn, a pleasant seventeenth-century public house, still flows.

Including those living in Bridgetown, on the east bank of the river by the bridge, there were about 4600 inhabitants of Totnes in 1800. Bridgetown, now a large suburb, was built as a new town away from the oldest area of Totnes in the twelfth century and a similar new town which was less successful, called Ford, may have been built in the vicinity of the present railway station. In about 1720, Daniel Defoe visited the town and commented upon the fine stone bridge and the Seven Stars Hotel, at which he stayed. This is still there and other travellers like John Swete have also remarked on the good food and lodging they enjoyed there. In 1828 the old bridge was too narrow and a new one was built at a cost of £12000 raised by subscription. The Duke of Somerset was responsible for providing steps to what is now called Vire Island and laying it out as a garden. He also built some pleasant houses in Bridgetown, and it was at this time that the Seymour Hotel was constructed. The foundations of the old bridge are still visible upstream of the new one.

Payne painted the bridge at Totnes, the Seven Stars and Mill beyond well before the burst of expansion at Bridgetown. The ship being loaded is probably moored close to where trips down the Dart start today. Not only Defoe but later travellers who visited the town were able to watch the capture of salmon peal – small salmon about 17–20 inches long – by a trap built in the mill leat which allowed the fish in whilst the tide was full, but at low tide left them stranded in only 12–18 inches of water. A well-trained dog was used to drive them into a waiting net which could collect thirty or so salmon at a time.

From the castle at the top of the town the view along the river in each direction and to the countryside beyond is particularly grand. In the past the town was regarded as the centre of the South Hams, and when local government was reorganized in 1974 the new South Hams District Council set up its offices here; these are now in Follaton House.

The fertile farms around the town were as valued in 1800 as they are now. Gilpin commented, 'Here the acre fills the bushels with abundant increase; and here the ox does credit to his pasture. But though the country abounds in corn and pasturage, cyder is its staple.' As a comment on the style of farming and the way of life around Totnes in 1800 this could hardly be bettered. The weekly markets for farm produce and the cattle markets held once a month marked its prosperity. The beauty of the countryside and its affluence, as well as the fine scenery of the Dart with its creeks below the town, ensured that Totnes remained a place of distinction with prosperous mansions both in and out of the town.

Two representatives were sent to Parliament from Totnes whilst Dartmouth sent only one. In the first thirty years of the century, before the Reform Act, the greatest number of electors polled was 75, only the Corporation and freemen having the right to vote. With a wider franchise after that date, about 300 had the vote, and of those 34 were freemen. Like other towns, Totnes had its charities and churches, almshouses and court where the borough magistrate held sway. In 1810 a library was opened in Fore Street, and the grammar-school, as well as a charity school in Bay Horse Street, provided a basic education extended in 1813 when a national school was opened. It was a self-sufficient town which by 1850 even had a dancing master, John Old of Fore Street, to introduce the artistic tradition still found here.

Totnes Bridge

Dartinton

Brent Bridge

Buckfastleigh Abbey

In 1984 a new bypass was built round the town and a new bridge spans the Dart, giving a raw view of the industrial estate unattractively littering the further bank before rejoining the old road beyond it. The road northwards to Dartington follows the west bank of the Dart and an old water-mill used by Dartington Hall Tweed is a picturesque reminder of earlier days. Dartington Hall itself has a delightful setting and is run by the Dartington Trust for educational and artistic purposes. In 1800 it was owned by the Champernowne family, who were lords of the manor. The Hall and the old retainers' buildings form two sides of a quadrangle, with the entrance buildings and Devon Centre making up the others. It has all the magnificence of a medieval palace, and the retainers' quarters, which have a series of entrance staircases jutting forward to allow separate accommodation upstairs and down, enhance the feeling. It is one of very few buildings in Devon to have a hammer-beam roof. The Elmhirsts, who set up the Dartington Trust in 1930, developed the estate on experimental lines for the benefit of the rural economy. They succeeded in supporting and developing rural crafts, as well as restoring the ancient manor buildings.

At the rear of the quadrangle are the gardens and the jousting green, flanked on the Hall side by large clipped yews shaped like enormous skittles, whilst on the opposite side the rising ground is terraced. Ilex oak, Scots pine, and a well-laid-out garden complement the grey stone buildings. The weir on the Dart is prominent but there must have been fewer trees in the parkland in 1800, since the buildings are now hidden from this spot.

Beyond Dartington is Buckfastleigh, which was a woollen centre at the beginning of the nineteenth century with 1500 inhabitants. It produced serges and had four mills although by 1850 two were empty. Two streams flow to the Dart here and this was good for combers to wash their wool. Another source of employment was the limestone quarries, including those that produced black marble. The countryside around the town was also renowned for the quantity and quality of its cider and cider orchards. This was still so throughout the first half of the nineteenth century, although the Cider Tax of 1763 reduced the amount made and growth of orchards. It is recorded that in one particularly happy year an acre of trees at Buckfastleigh had produced 4000 gallons.

The legacy of the industrial past in Buckfastleigh is several large factories along the river banks. They include some of the ugliest industrial buildings in Devon today, but their connection with wool and the woollen industry persists. In the older part of this small town, where Fore Street, Chapel Street and Plymouth Road meet, the roads are narrow and curved, two- or three-storey buildings edge the pavements, and the building line is uneven. Different building materials and colour-washed houses are mixed with the intriguing sight of cottages where families once lived on the ground and first floors whilst the upper floors were used for woollen manufacture.

Buckfast Abbey was originally an extensive place founded in 1137 for monks of the Cistercian order, but after it was dissolved by Henry VIII the building fell into ruins, which in 1806 had been largely cleared away. The stone was used for building elsewhere, and only after the First World War was the Abbey rebuilt. It now supports a community of Benedictine monks and attracts tourists, who purchase mead and honey and enjoy the beauty of the place – quite a contrast with Payne's romantic picture of a ruin.

Brixham & Berryhead from Tor Wood

Payne's paintings of Torbay vividly illustrate the county's unspoilt natural charm. A distant view of Brixham and Berry Head avoids any hint of houses or people in an area which today is crowded. About 113000 now live in the Borough of Torbay, but in 1800 Brixham's seafaring population of about 3700 was equal in size to the population of all the surrounding villages put together. Napoleon, on board the *Bellerophon* before transferring to the *Northumberland* on his way to St Helena, thought Torbay was as beautiful as the Bay of Naples, with its blue sky, rocks, sand and enticing green hills beyond. Holiday-makers and newcomers wishing to live there followed the earlier trend begun at Exmouth.

The coastline between Kingswear and Sharkham Point, south of Brixham, has kept its remote rural beauty. Parts are protected by the National Trust, who own Coleton Fishacre and its coastal estate. Coleton Fishacre is a large house built in 1925 and designed by Roger Milne for the D'Oyly Carte family, who between 1925 and 1940 created its gardens. In the early years, when artistic friends of the family were invited to house parties some of them enjoyed sunbathing in the nude on the remote lawns. The gardening staff were told to keep their minds on their work, which with commendable strength of will they did, creating the fine garden which is now open to the public. The house is in private use and out of the holiday season enjoys the quietness once common along the whole of Devon's coasts.

On the estate, by the coastal path, are the formidable remains of a coastal defence battery from the Second World War, and grand views along the coast with its dramatic cliffs and sandy beaches.

Scabbacombe Sands, Long Sands and Man Sands have always been considered as good as any bathing beaches in the country. Beyond Sharkham Point, modern Brixham marries what were two separate villages, Upper and Lower Brixham, still called locally Cow Town and Fish Town. In 1966 Brixham became part of Torbay Borough, although separated from Paignton by a welcome strip of countryside. By 1800 two fortifications had been built on Berry Head at Brixham, the most easterly part of Torbay. This rocky promontory is now a country park which boasts the shortest lighthouse in the country, and is run by the Borough Council. During the Napoleonic Wars up to 1000 men were garrisoned there. One or two military buildings and the fortifications, with a remarkable stone sentry-box, are still here. To produce a warlike effect ancient cannon have been placed in the embrasures so that a ghostly sentry in his stone box can feel suitably at home.

At the turn of the eighteenth century Brixham's importance was particularly great as a shelter for the Fleet, which came to the bay when westerly winds turned to gales. Naval ships obtained water from reservoirs built here in 1801 for the Navy. It is possible that Brixham people noted the irony of completing the work just as the peace treaty of Amiens was signed, although more probably they anticipated prosperity from the next war. In 1809, six years after it came, a military hospital was built here. When the war finally ended in 1815 this became a private house, and later a hotel.

Brixham's prosperity came mainly from a fishing fleet of a hundred sail, one of the largest in the kingdom. The harbour with a new quay was completed in 1804, but it was soon realized that it would have to be enlarged if it were to shelter all the boats that wished to berth here. By 1840 a new pier and breakwater to shelter a great number of larger merchantmen and naval frigates had been planned, and building work began in 1844. The size of ships at Brixham grew from an average of about 60–70 tons at the beginning of the century until in 1850 there were six brigs of about 170 tons, 140 schooners of 60–180 tons and 130 fishing smacks of 30–50 tons, as well as 80 open boats used for hook fishing.

One of the pleasures of the sea is watching fishing vessels returning to harbour to unload their catch. When the importance of Brixham as a fishing port was at its height during the first half of the nineteenth century, the quay would be heaped with turbot, sole, whiting, plaice, mullet, gurnet, flounders, herrings, etc., which were sold by a local type of Dutch auction, with the prime lots invariably sent to Exeter, Bristol, Bath, London or elsewhere. At this time the coastal and Mediterranean trade, which had either been restricted or lapsed entirely during the French wars, was revived.

The harbour, like that of Torquay, drained with the tide. In Brixham this left a muddy and smelly basin which was 'by no means agreeable to mere landsmen'. Added to this the fishing town itself was amongst the dirtiest along the coast. As time passed, many of the wealthier citizens moved from the harbour area up to the surrounding hillsides to avoid the squalor as well as the vigorous and bawdy behaviour of Brixham's fisherfolk. The harbour today seems remote from this with a good working atmosphere, neat shops nearby and quaint cottages above it on the hill. The fishermen now belong to a co-operative and there is no longer a ritual auction.

This hardy community was regarded as spiritually rather threadbare at the end of the eighteenth century. An example of this was the great antagonism to letting Nonconformists build chapels. There was some outright persecution of, and difficulty for, the Baptists and nobody would sell or give them land for a chapel. Consequently they bought their own small quarry and after a struggle built their chapel in 1801. No doubt recognizing the value of building on rock, the Methodists acquired the quarry site from the Baptists, and in 1816 built a chapel in Fore Street. Not until 1820 was an Anglican church built in the Lower Town as a chapel of ease, although the parish church of the Virgin Mary with its lofty battlemented tower had served for centuries in the Upper Town.

There were the normal charities in Brixham, for the poor, elderly and needy. One typical bequest by John Kelland benefited the school. In 1712 he left £2000 for charitable purposes in Devon, part of which was used to buy a farm in Ashburton for the support of a schoolmaster at Brixham, who as a condition of his employment had to teach reading, writing, arithmetic and navigation. This last subject must have been a rare one for pupils, but in a seafaring spot like Brixham it was obviously a useful one.

North-west of Brixham were the firm sands of Paignton. Like those elsewhere in the bay they were free from the numerous holiday-makers that enjoy them today. Paignton was less than half the size of Brixham and its centre lay up the hill around the red sandstone church of St John, about a mile from the sea. Beside the churchyard, which is a pleasant sheltered spot enclosed by large stone walls, are the remains of the Priory, unchanged since Payne's day. Close by is Kirkham House, which was built in medieval times and could have been one of the Priory's buildings. It was restored by the Department of the Environment and is open to the public. Built of red stone and slate, it contrasts with nearby modern buildings whose scale and quality are less attractive.

The area close to the church in Paignton is becoming increasingly attractive. Nearby is the nineteenth-century former brewery, restored in 1983 by the Devon Historic Buildings Trust and kept as part of a neat housing development completed by the Borough Council. Victorian buildings in the area give an attractive feeling, not least because the streets are narrow and winding. Many of the buildings are quaintly old fashioned and the area is less affluent than it deserves to be.

Only after 1850 did Paignton start to expand rapidly, whilst Torquay had grown in elegance and wealth earlier in the century. At the beginning of the nineteenth century Paignton was renowned for growing large cabbages and making good cider, which was loaded on to coastal vessels and sent to London. Not until 1838 was a pier built. It cost about £5000 and was used by vessels of up to 150 tons. As ships became larger and rail and road transport improved, it lost its commercial attraction and today is used for holiday amusements. Together with the Festival Theatre, built in 1966, it helps support Paignton as a holiday resort that has grown continuously since the coming of the railway.

The market held at Paignton in 1800 was as well stocked with fish and local produce grown on its rich red soil as neighbouring Brixham's. Paignton had various charities and a school where the schoolmaster was paid to teach all the basic subjects and how to 'cast accounts'. Other schools were built as the town grew. For some years the needs of fishing and farming were supported by the trades of the town in a simple and direct way altered only as the new demands of holiday-makers increased.

The most outstanding building in the bay belonged to the Cary family, who had come to Torquay in 1662 and lived in Abbey House, which was relatively new at the end of the eighteenth century. It had been built with two wings protruding from the main front towards the sea, and it was thought to be one of the best-sited houses in the county. Its grounds rose slightly in front but still allowed fine seaward views from the family rooms, which were on the first floor. From here the Carys were able to watch the Fleet entering the bay under sail as well as the red-sailed Brixham trawlers passing about their business.

Beside the house were the remains of the Abbey and an ancient tithe barn clad in ivy. Legend had it that many years before Spaniards had landed, intent on plundering the Abbey, but had been taken by surprise by the English Fleet arriving unexpectedly and had been put to flight. It was said that they had

Payngton Sands

Torr Abbey from Torquay

taken refuge in the grey stone buttressed barn and had been starved to death there. Certainly some kind of action took place by the barn, and the museum now housed in Abbey House exhibits cannon shot found embedded in its walls.

The grounds of the house were extensive and planted with avenues, some of which were mature. Elm and oak of considerable age were amongst the trees which graced them. Around the house were fields and woods with rocky cliffs and rolling hills, which as the town grew to 9000 inhabitants by 1850 were built on. The older part of the town and the tradesmen's houses were close to the harbour, whilst on the hills overlooking the valleys and the bay neat terraces and villas were built using the local limestone. Within fifty years rows of houses climbed the hills, hiding the rural charm but creating an attractive town with open space and gardens, sometimes planted with palms or other exotic plants.

Payne's painting of Torquay with the old pier and various ships is particularly attractive, showing its scale before it grew. The trading vessels brought coal, timber and other merchandise to the town whilst barges took limestone quarried at Berry Head along the coast to the Exe, and larger vessels had some trade with Newfoundland. Only in 1803 was building undertaken to enclose a harbour basin 500 feet by 300 feet with piers and a quay, which was unfinished for some years.

In order to recruit builders for the new harbour, advertisements were posted throughout Devon with the necessary postscript that those working on the project would be protected from the press-gang. However attractive the sight of the Fleet coming into Torbay might have been for the Carys, for many it was a constant reminder of enforced service with the Royal Navy and the corruption and brutality of the Senior Service.

In 1803, when war with France resumed, the guarantee was particularly pertinent. The maxim of those in the press-gangs enforcing recruitment, who were paid a bounty per head, was that force should be used only if resistance was met. In 1778 a midshipman engaged in a press-gang accidentally killed a Torbay fisherman. His punishment was as brutal as his own behaviour, and he was sentenced 'to be burnt in the hand which was done immediately'. Branding as a punishment was intended to label a villain, and had remained a deterrent since the sixteenth century.

The recruitment of criminals from gaols was common. In another local context, ringleaders of those who had been plundering the brig *St Peter*, which went aground in Torbay in 1771, were shipped aboard a man-of-war as punishment rather than being imprisoned. It may well have been an infinitely worse fate than prison, and since the Fleet took care to anchor in deep water, and to have a boat manned by redcoated marines with rifles keeping a look-out for deserters, the chances of returning to shore were limited. The same happened after the war, when in 1823 John Lake and John Tizzard were committed to the County Gaol for offences against the customs and sentenced to be impressed to the Navy.

Tor Quay

The Fleet was of considerable interest to the people of Devon, who watched developments and possibly prospered by them. Until the last quarter of the eighteenth century there had been few alterations to the basic design of sailing ships for centuries, although they had gradually grown larger. The needs of the French wars started to transform the Navy. The largest ships at the turn of the century were those with 100 guns on three decks, but by 1820 the most powerful had 120 guns. These were known as first-rate vessels, and were expensive to maintain and keep at sea, as were the second-rate vessels, carrying 90–98 guns. Some third-rate ships had three decks and 80 guns, but most had two decks carrying 64, 70 or 74 guns. These three largest types of ships were regarded as ships of the line and able to take part in battles against the best fleets of France and Spain, although the enemy tended to have larger ships, particularly in the first half of the eighteenth century.

The fifth- or sixth-rate ships, with 32–44 guns or 20–28 guns carried on one deck except for a few which had 44 guns on two decks, were used as escort vessels. Frigates with 28, 32 or 36 guns were used for individual patrols and scouting, and were first engaged in action in the mid-eighteenth century. By 1790 there were larger frigates with 40 or 44 guns, and this gradual increase in firepower continued until 1820, when all frigates had 50 guns. A variety of other ships of all sizes were used by the Navy including schooners, which appeared in the 1760s, purchased from North America. In 1805 the schooner *Pickle*, chosen for speed, brought the Trafalgar despatches to Plymouth.

The British Ships at Trafalgar

Ships of the Line

Victory	101 guns	Conqueror	74 guns
Royal Sovereign	100 guns	Achilles	74 guns
Britannia	100 guns	Colossus	74 guns
Temeraire	98 guns	Defence	74 guns
Neptune	98 guns	Leviathan	74 guns
Prince	98 guns	Bellerophon	74 guns
Dreadnought	98 guns	Orion	74 guns
Tonnant	80 guns	Swiftsure	74 guns
Belleisle	74 guns	Ajax	74 guns
Revenge	74 guns	Thunderer	74 guns
Spartiate	74 guns	Polyphemus	64 guns
Mars	74 guns	Africa	64 guns
Defiance	74 guns	Agamemnon	64 guns
Monotaur	74 guns		

Frigates

Euryalus	36 guns
Naiad	36 guns
Phoebe	36 guns
Sirius	36 guns

Cutter

Entreprenante	10 guns

Schooner

Pickle	10 guns

The cutters and schooners were maids of all work used to service the Fleet, for despatches, moving men or scouting. Cutters were quite small, about 720 feet long with a beam of 25 feet, and had a gaff-rigged mainsail.

In addition to the growth in size, other developments were either forced upon the Navy or were a natural response to needs. There were gradual changes in the rigging of ships as well as the size of armaments. The wooden hulls of the Fleet were built of oak, and shipbuilders preferred it to come from the Weald of Sussex and Surrey. By the end of the eighteenth century, when a third-rate ship needed about 3000 trees, oak was becoming too expensive because the large plantations of the seventeenth century had been felled. Throughout the eighteenth century elm, beech and fir were used, and at the turn of the century teak was introduced. After the treaty in 1807 between France, Russia and Prussia to blockade the Baltic, from which oak timber and plank, fir masts, pitch and turpentine had been acquired, more naval stores came from the New England colonies, although convoys of up to 500 ships still brought some supplies from the Baltic. In turn, shipbuilding skills were developed in the colonies to provide a cheaper alternative to the established shipyards in England.

Another difficulty was that wood-boring worms introduced from tropical waters attacked the oak hulls of the Fleet, so during the early eighteenth century the main hull was sheathed in planking laid over coal-tar and hair. After 1778 copper sheeting was used instead of the planking, but the galvanic action between copper and iron bolt-heads created problems which after 1783 were solved by using hardened copper–zinc fastenings. By the end of the century most warships were being bottomed in copper to preserve the expensive oak hulls.

Towards the end of the war Sir Robert Seppings, Surveyor of the Navy between 1813 and 1832, introduced ship designs employing timber of smaller dimensions than was traditional. By 1804 the square bow on the middle deck of men-of-war had been remodelled to a round one, to eliminate its weakness, and by 1817 the round stern had been introduced to give an increased arc of fire as well as strength. The most important innovation was the use of steam, the first steam-powered man-of-war, *U.S.S. Fulton*, being commissioned on 29 October 1814 in New York. By the 1830s steam had been introduced commercially and into the Royal Navy.

On a par with some of the warships were the largest trading vessels of the East India Company, carrying cannon and a bigger crew than most trading ships, which employed as few sailors as possible to lower costs. In 1800 most East Indiamen were about the size of a third-rate vessel, around 400–500 tons and 140 feet long, and armed against pirates with 30 guns. By 1820 they had generally doubled in size. Of the normal trading vessels, in 1780 there were a few two-masted ships of 200 tons, but most above this size were three masted and square rigged. In 1788, 80% of the vessels registered were less than 200 tons. Possibly the most common types of overseas trading ship were the two-masted brigs, brigantines and schooners, with different types of sail.

Most merchant ships were small boats engaged in coastal trade that used navigable rivers like the Exe, Dart or Taw and Torridge. They carried coal, timber, salt, vegetables and various types of general merchandise, like the sharpening stones quarried from the Blackdown Hills and exported elsewhere in the country. In 1800 these numerous ships varied in construction, rigging and sail and were frequently from 20 to 50 tons. There were boatbuilding firms on most of Devon's estuaries, each serving the needs of local merchants and particular trades. Barges, ketches, schooners and lighters were found everywhere.

Comparable Larger Ships, 1794
Source: H.M.S.O.

	Royal Navy: 80-gun ship	*Merchant Fleet: Indiaman*
Length	182 ft	165 ft 6½ in.
Maximum beam	49 ft	42 ft
Depth of hold	21 ft	17 ft
Tonnage (burthen)	1955	1257

Whilst there were improved ships and armaments, the conditions of service in the Royal Navy between 1793 and 1815 were appalling. Methods of maintaining discipline had hardly changed since 1740, when Peter White of the Hood was court-martialled for desertion and received twenty lashes on his bare back alongside each of the three flagships and forty alongside *Torbay*, the ship on which he served. The reputations of commanders like Lord St Vincent for brutal treatment of their men created great resentment towards the Navy and its supporting press-gangs. Corned beef and biscuit with wine and water, all of the poorest quality, were the standard rations for those serving in the Navy, which helped fuel the resentment. The contractors victualling the Navy were ruthless in exploiting the war and servicemen.

It is hardly surprising that a mutiny at Spithead in 1797 spread to Plymouth, where the red flag flew from every masthead. This premeditated act resulted in an increase of one shilling a day being promised to the sailors, and no arrests were to be made. But at Portsmouth the Admiralty went back on its promise, and arrested ringleaders. Able Seaman Parker, who came from Exeter and had once served as a midshipman, then left the Navy only to re-enlist as an ordinary seaman, led the gravest mutiny, at the Nore. At Plymouth, officers were turned out of their ships, and some were placed on wooden gratings to be towed ashore. Others were less fortunate and dipped into the harbour trussed from the yards. The spirit of revenge and opportunism encouraged mobs in Plymouth to plunder homes of officials. There was panic and demands for law and order to be quickly restored.

Retribution followed with ringleaders flogged and executed at the Nore, Spithead and Plymouth. At Plymouth the Admiral, Lord Keith, had a list of 50 sailors who were eventually to be made scapegoats for those involved in the mutiny. There were fourteen executions and the remainder were flogged.

If the sight of Torbay, stretching from Berry Head in the south to Hope's Nose in the north, was awe inspiring and inviting to the tourist, it must have appeared a haven of tranquillity to those on board the battleships. The sandy coves, the grey limestone rocks rising abruptly at either end and the well-wooded slopes of many of the hills presented a picture that many artists could not resist. The presence of the Fleet encouraged wives and friends to visit the bay, and enticed by the beauty of the coast and mild weather they sometimes stayed. Exmouth had first started to develop in the 1760s and had slowly grown in popularity. By contrast Torquay, with 1000 inhabitants in 1800, grew to 9000 by 1850, by which time St Marychurch had become a suburb and the village of Torre engulfed by the spread of houses.

Visitors who dared could explore not only the rural charms of Babbacombe, Cockington and Marldon but also the caves at Kent's Hole. These had been known for generations and had been worn from the limestone by water or created by prehistoric man. There were two openings midway up a steep cliff and the more accessible led into a passage which introduced the explorer into several large caves. They are more grandly known as Kent's Cavern today and modern tourists have a less precarious opportunity to see the stalagmites and stalactites in all their interesting colours – greys, greens and reds. Modern lighting, further excavations to allow easier access, and guides to point out the interesting sights allow even greater pleasure for many more people. From the 1860s the caves have become steadily more popular, and the remains of prehistoric animals are now carefully displayed in the tourist shop and museum at their entrance.

The earliest travellers around Torbay invariably visited Compton Castle, built by Sir Maurice de Pole in Henry II's time, and the romantic remains of Berry Pomeroy Castle, built in the early fourteenth century. By the turn of the eighteenth century Compton Castle was in a parlous condition and part of the building was occupied by a farmer. Later it changed hands and in the 1820s was lived in by a Mr Templer, who made it habitable. Some visitors felt that the alterations were not harmonious with the picturesque and ancient building, but its machicolated gateways and towers continued to attract visitors. In 1850 Mr Francis Garrett of Parkfield House was the owner and his gardener lived there. In more recent times the property was repurchased and restored by the Gilbert family, who had owned it centuries earlier. To the great credit of the late Commander Walter Raleigh Gilbert and his wife, the property is now in the hands of the National Trust, who open it to the public, selling mementos from the thatched stone barn in front.

Berry Pomeroy Castle started to fall into decay at the start of the eighteenth century when Sir Edward Seymour left it to live in Wiltshire. By the end of the century it had fallen into ruin, but it was in such a delightful spot, close to the sea and the sylvan beauties of Torbay, that it attracted curious and romantic tourists. The great gate and walls of the southern front, one or two turrets and some apartments on the west side were the most substantial remains. Trees were growing close to the walls and overhanging them, ivy climbed the walls, and moss and lichen tinged them with green so that they presented an attractive relic of bygone days even then. The ruins, which are still magnificent, overlook the Gatcombe Brook as it flows beneath the northern walls along the widening valley.

Close by in this attractive rolling countryside, two villages about the same size as Torquay in 1800, Broadhempston with 670 inhabitants and Ipplepen with 820, retained their charm and relative isolation until the 1950s. Recent expansion of Newton Abbot and Torquay and the mobility of modern times have more than doubled Ipplepen's population. Within Torbay, Cockington

Berry Pomeroy Castle

still keeps the essence of a tiny village with its stone and thatch, much as it was at the beginning of the nineteenth century.

To the east beyond Babbacombe, the rocky cliffs drop down to the Teign Estuary and the fishing village of Shaldon, with nearby Ringmore, on the south side of the river. At the turn of the eighteenth century their total population was about 800, but like East and West Teignmouth they had been discovered. Shaldon doubled its population to over 1250 in the first fifty years of the century, and with the building of the bridge across the Teign in 1826/7 gradually became regarded as a suburb of Teignmouth.

The attractions for those wishing to settle or holiday in the village were its fine beach, hilly scenery and red sandstone cliffs. It still feels like a self-contained village, with its old cottages around Myddle Street, and it is possible to enjoy the early development at Marine Terrace and Clifford Place. There is a good view across the harbour to Teignmouth, from which a ferry runs to Shaldon.

Teignmouth & Exmouth,
the Parson and Clerk, looking eastward

The iron and wood bridge built in 1826/7 was the longest in the country at that time, measuring 557 yards with 34 arches. Previously, the ferry took horses and traps across the water, with the consequent delay if there were unfavourable winds or seas. The bridge was largely rebuilt in 1838 and reopened in 1840. East and West Teignmouth were parted by a brook running between them, and totalled about 2000 inhabitants in 1800. By 1850 Teignmouth was a single town and had grown 2½ times as large.

When Payne painted East Teignmouth and the sandy beach with a rider approaching from the direction of Torquay, it was quite free of the villas and terraces that were built later. It was a fishing port also exporting ball clay dug up in the Bovey area for use in pottery and pipes. The shifting sand-bar at the entrance to the estuary is still hazardous for the large clay-coasters that leave the quay. The Newfoundland trade employed 20 ships from Teignmouth and Shaldon which ranged from 50 to 200 tons in the last part of the eighteenth century, and provided employment for many people up to the middle of the nineteenth century.

The development of the Stover Canal to encourage trade through Teignmouth started in 1790. Thomas Gray, who was Surveyor to Exeter Corporation, was the engineer in charge of the work. It was intended that the canal should run from the Teign at Newton Abbot to Bovey Tracey, but it stretched for only two miles north, as far as Ventiford near Teigngrace. The work was completed in 1792 and the canal prospered. Ball clay was shipped to the Potteries via the Liverpool and Trent–Mersey Canal, and in 1798 James Templer, who had financed the Stover Canal, won an order from the Wedgwood Company. Ten barges were used to take the clay along the canal and Teign Estuary together with lignite and iron ore found nearby. Coal, manure, limestone and sea-sand were brought back up the canal from Teignmouth. In 1820 George Templer, who had inherited his father's eye for business as well as the estate at Stover, introduced a granite tramway connecting quarries at Holwell and Haytor to the canal at Ventiford, and went on to build the New Quay at Teignmouth.

Haytor granite was used in the rebuilding of London Bridge in 1825. It could have been this order that had encouraged George Templer to develop the tramway and New Quay. As well as for kerbstones and other mundane engineering uses, granite was provided for the British Museum and National Gallery.

The fishery of Teignmouth caught large quantities of salmon, salmon peal, sea trout, whiting and mackerel. A local regulation required fish caught here to be offered in the first instance to any local people who were prepared to buy at the market price, before it was offered for sale elsewhere. At Shaldon there were eight nets for salmon fishing and this was done by women who dressed in baggy trousers, like the Dutch. It was not uncommon for one sweep of the nets to catch a dozen salmon in this well-stocked river. The Dean and Chapter of Exeter received tithes on all fish caught and this continued after the Tithes Commutation Act of 1836. This Act required the contribution of a

Stover Lodge

East Teignmouth

tenth of produce from the earth, which provided the Church with its income, to be commuted to an agreed monetary payment. In 1791/2 Pitt had felt it unwise to introduce commutation as too radical a step, but by 1820 changing types of agriculture, enclosure and the need for the Church to reform made it desirable. By 1830 commutation had already happened by mutual agreement in most places including the parishes of Devon, where between two shillings and sixpence and three shillings in the pound on rent was paid. In some counties like Bedfordshire, Kent, Lincolnshire and Shropshire, though, the tithe barns were still filled with produce.

A good number of attractive houses had been built by 1815 and produced some pleasant terraces. The Den is a fine open space fronted by some good early nineteenth-century buildings, and the shops in the roads running back from it supply the needs of the townspeople today much as they did when Keats and Fanny Burney stayed in Teignmouth to enjoy its modern facilities. By 1820 Teignmouth was well known, attracting many to its sandy, gently sloping beach and bathing-machines. A range of hot baths had been attached to the main hotels for the benefit of invalids, and there were reading-rooms and a library. The town's picturesque setting encouraged more people to holiday and settle here during the rest of the century.

In and around the town there are also some outstanding buildings like Bitton House, owned by Teignbridge District Council, with its recently restored orangery. Its gardens are now well used by the public, and its setting and scale are similar to those of other contemporary buildings of the well-to-do. It was once the home of Admiral Pelew, who later became Lord Exmouth and had achieved distinction by laying siege to Algiers in 1816. His success is permanently marked by two cannon captured there.

Shipbuilding no longer takes place at Teignmouth although during the French wars it supplied warships like the 484 ton sloop *Talbot*, with 18 guns. She was completed in 1807, commanded by the Hon. A. Jones on the Lisbon station between 1807 and 1809, and was finally stationed in the West Indies in 1814, before being sold a year later. A multitude of small pleasure craft now use the harbour, and the ball-clay ships dwarf the more homely yachts, as they pass over the bar bound for foreign ports.

Beside the Teign towards Newton Abbot, Bishopsteignton in 1800 was a village straggling along the road with beautiful views of the water and hills beyond. Fewer than 700 people lived there but it had all the normal trades and shops necessary to sustain a small farming community. The Revd John Comyns was the patron and incumbent of the vicarage from 1801 until 1856. Like many others of the squirearchy he owned the tithes and much of the parish, as well as being the lord of the manors of Bishopsteignton and Radway. He enjoyed a comfortable life and had a pleasant mansion called Wood House about a mile and a half from the ancient church of St John. It had six bells then hung in a central tower, which was crowned with a shingled spire. The tower was rebuilt in 1815 at the west end. Bishopsteignton had the curacy of West Teignmouth attached to it, reflecting the relative importance of the two communities at the time, although in 1822/3 East and West Teignmouth Churches were both rebuilt.

Kingsteignton, closer to Newton Abbot, was equally well sited and a little larger than Bishopsteignton. During the next fifty years it doubled in size, owing to the importance of ball-clay exports, which amounted to 50 000 tons per year, employing about 200 miners. The Church of St Michael was already old in 1801 when the decayed rood-screen was removed. The village has grown and is becoming a suburb of Newton Abbot.

At the turn of the eighteenth century Newton Abbot was an ancient market-town separated by the River Lemon from Newton Bushel, once a rival medieval new town. The market in Newton Bushel was stopped when the markets and fairs of Newton Abbot came under the same ownership of the Yarde family. The market-town atmosphere, captured in the newly remodelled and rebuilt market in Newton Abbot centre, still epitomizes the promise of country produce, good humour and the renewal of friendships forged whilst trading there. With the cattle market it keeps the age-old traditions which existed when its population was around 2000 at the end of the eighteenth century.

Most building followed the arrival of the railway around 1850. St Leonard's Tower is preserved in the centre and some older Tudor buildings remain, but the most interesting properties are Forde House, built in 1610 by Sir Richard Reynell and now the offices of Teignbridge District Council, and Bradley Manor to the south-west of the town, probably built during the fifteenth century.

Along the coast, Dawlish was attracting people before 1800, with its red cliffs, rolling hills and golden-brown sands. In 1795 the cost of renting a house for a week at the height of the season was two guineas, compared with less than half a guinea twenty years earlier. When the Revd John Swete brought his family here to get over inoculation against smallpox and his own attacks of rheumatism, he enjoyed the Lawn running along the bottom of the valley to the beach unimpaired by the railway line which in 1844 was built on a viaduct across the mouth of the valley by the South Devon Railway. Whatever the architectural quality of Brunel's station, it had little to commend it from the point of view of those living on either side of the Lawn.

The houses gradually spread back from the sea in the first fifty years of the century, and many of those facing the Lawn had been built by 1809. At the turn of the century the little stream along the valley bottom had been channelled to flow in a series of pleasant waterfalls as it does today. Nearby was a large overshot water-wheel which attracted passers-by just as its equally large and impressive successor does. Langstone Rock at the north-east end of the bay and the impressive Parson and Clerk rocks at the base of the high red cliffs to the south-west have always been inspiring and worthy of paintings like Payne's.

The church was picturesquely sited about a mile inland, away from the earliest houses and later connected by continuous development. It was an

Dawlish

ancient building but was rebuilt except for its tower in 1824/5. The spate of earlier development was kept within the confines of the valley, and more-recent building has been beyond the steep hills that flank the older centre without destroying the old atmosphere of this pleasant seaside town. Only the public toilets, provided in unsightly prominence on the Lawn, are truly unpleasant, although for some tastes this attractive open space is rather too cluttered with lights and other paraphernalia.

The attraction and distinction of the town around 1800 is reflected in Luscombe Castle (formerly Luscombe Park), designed by the eminent architect John Nash for Sir S. R. E. Hoare of Stourhead, a leading banker, with grounds laid out by the equally renowned landscape designer Repton. It is situated in one of the most pleasant valleys in the Haldon range and had a variety of quiet countryside views. It took four years to build and has a combination of towers, battlements, pinnacles and mullioned windows. Inside it had a variety of excellent paintings, sculptures and an organ in the staircase hall, together with a library of valuable books. The large Gothic conservatory housed rare and exotic plants and the Gothic style in the rest of the house was evident in its windows and porch. There were moulded plaster ceilings, stained-glass windows and fine marble fireplaces. Perhaps one should not be surprised by such quality, or that in 1862 a chapel was added by the famous architect Sir Gilbert Scott. Dawlish attracted only the best in its early years of fashionable growth.

Although the Gothic style is found in many buildings within the town, nothing can quite match Luscombe Castle or Stonelands, another Nash house, built around 1805. Some attractive houses in Plantation Terrace were put up at this time, overlooking the Lawn and the busy little shops that face either side. Excellent cider and a plethora of mackerel, herring and other fish provided ideal opportunities for gourmets to taste basic Devonshire fare at the turn of the eighteenth century.

The Exe Estuary

In 1800 Exeter was a pleasant small market-town with a population of about 20 000, similar in size to present-day Barnstaple. The mayor, twenty-four aldermen, four bailiffs, a recorder, chamberlain, sheriff and town clerk ran the city, which was a county in its own right and sent two members to Parliament. Only freemen and freeholders were given the opportunity to vote at elections, so that the franchise was limited to the more prosperous.

Exeter had grown up on a high ridge which contemporary observers suggested was healthy because of its salubrious airs. A view of Payne's from Rougemont Castle, where the County Courts were built in 1773, shows the estuary in full flood with Topsham, hardly visible, beside it. Beneath the castle walls there appears to be little but the billowing tops of trees, without a sign of the Cathedral or spires of churches. Present-day views from just below the walls in Rougemont Gardens, behind the City Library, are by no means as rural, and buildings stretch away southwards interspersed only occasionally by mature trees. Certainly by 1800 buildings had spread well beyond the city walls, and vacant plots and orchards that had been a feature of earlier times were being built over.

The Castle stood in the north-east part of the city and looked down in every direction on the old city walls, the remains of which are still there. Most of the earliest buildings grew up along High Street and Fore Street, a continuous road a mile and a half long cut in two by North Street and South Street, as it is today. To the south of High Street is the Cathedral, dedicated to St Peter, with its massive bulk and twin towers that have dominated Exeter since the twelfth century. In 1763 it had been thoroughly repaired and redecorated, probably in a similar way to that started several years ago and still continuing. A new window was placed over the west door in 1766. Since medieval times the west

Exe, Topsham from Exeter Castle

Exeter

front has presented a magnificent stone screen to the Cathedral Close, with the lower part ornamented with carvings of apostles, kings, crusaders, etc.

The Cathedral was shown by Payne in a rural scene painted from St Thomas, and with the red Devon cows ruminating placidly by the water could hardly be more evocative of the county town even today. An Act of Parliament in 1769 had authorized the building of the New Exe Bridge to replace the medieval one. Work started in 1770 but as it was nearing completion the bridge was destroyed by a flood, and not finished until 1778. Eventually this too was replaced, in 1905, and a picture by Rubens Southey (1880–1933) of the old grey stone bridge with three spans is displayed at Exeter's Victoria and Albert Museum. It was a simple bridge unlike the earlier medieval one, which had twenty-four spans, parts of which are preserved in gardens open to the public, and incorporated both red sandstone and white limestone, contrasting for effect.

A panoramic view across the city like that seen by Payne can be enjoyed from the higher part of the University grounds. Until the improved roads and coming of the railway in 1844, the estuary was the lifeline of the city and the area about it. Exeter prospered as a woollen-manufacturing centre, exporting its own goods and importing others needed for manufacturing or personal use through the quays of the Exe Estuary. The importance of Exeter and the port of Topsham to the county at the end of the eighteenth century is difficult to overestimate. Woollen goods from most parts of the county were exported from Exeter. The serge-manufacturing business was most important, and cloth produced as far away as Hatherleigh, Okehampton, Chagford, Moretonhampstead, Sandford, Crediton, Morchard Bishop, Honiton and Ottery St Mary came to the city. Exeter and Tiverton were the two centres where cloth which had been woven and fulled could be dressed, dyed, packed and despatched. Barnstaple and Bideford, like Dartmouth and Plymouth, exported small quantities of locally made cloth, but the skills and commercial contacts in Exeter, as well as its position, ensured its prosperity.

The period from 1790 to the end of the Napoleonic Wars was the last era when Exeter was a prosperous port for woollen exports. The war reduced opportunities to export to Europe and, unlike manufacturers elsewhere, the commercial community did not take their chances to export through neutral European ports. Instead prosperity was kept up by increased sales to the East India Company. In 1783 the Company took 35 000 pieces, each measuring 26 yards, but in 1800, 121 000 pieces worth £204 000 were sold. In 1810 this had increased to 200 000 pieces worth £300 000, many of them being sent 'white' to London, where they were dyed and pressed. The East India Company reduced their demand by half the following year and by 1822 only 350 people in Exeter and nearby were employed in the industry.

Amongst other goods sold through Exeter and despatched along the estuary were paper, leather materials and farm produce. In the eighteenth century seventeen paper-mills using the abundant water supplies for their power and processing raw material contributed to Exeter's wealth. The large number of cattle in east and central Devon, with oak bark plentiful for tanning, encouraged the leather trade, although later the port also became a centre for assembling raw materials for tanning when the demand for local wood outstripped supply.

Particularly during the Napoleonic Wars, there was considerable ship-building on the estuary, although because of the cost of transporting naval stores along the canal to the city, greater effort was put into repairing vessels than building them here. Associated with this, cord, rope, sailcloth and chain cables were all made in Exeter and sold to supply the requirements of boatbuilders or merchants here and elsewhere. In the city, there were iron foundries, corn-mills, malt-kilns, breweries and tanneries using the estuary for their transportation.

Although Exeter thrived because of the estuary, it also suffered because it was necessary to use the ancient canal, built in 1566, to bring goods up to the city. The canal was still a limitation even though it had been improved in 1676 and 1701. By the end of the eighteenth century larger vessels could use the canal only with difficulty and so they either unloaded on the quays of Topsham or transferred their loads to smaller lighters, which were not hampered by the canal being only 9 feet deep. In 1827 the canal was further improved by being extended two miles to Turf below Topsham, where locks were built, and the depth was increased throughout its length to take vessels of 14 foot draught. For some time this made the new quays of Exeter more competitive but inevitably larger ships became fashionable, and competition from railways and improved roads destroyed the advantages gained by these improvements. In 1865 the development of Exmouth Dock, which was connected with the railway, further weakened Exeter's attraction as a port.

The canal posed navigational problems and difficulties for traders sending the region's wares direct from Exeter to other parts of the world, or along the coast to London, Plymouth or Bristol, but the estuary was not much better. It was the only navigable estuary for large ships between Lyme Regis and Dartmouth and so prospered up to the early part of the nineteenth century. But although the estuary is up to a mile wide at Starcross and is attractive to look at in full flood, at low water it has narrow channels suitable only for small boats. Furthermore, getting through the mouth of the estuary from the sea required skilled navigation to deal with a restricted entry, winds, tides and a clearance of only 6 feet at low water, often resulting in delays. This contrasted badly with either Dartmouth or Plymouth, both of which had more than 28 feet at a time when the largest vessels required only 12 feet of water.

Whatever its navigational limitations, the estuary is still exceptionally attractive. Its use by weekend sailors, fishermen and walkers enjoying the birdlife, for which it has become particularly well known, has changed it from the commercial thoroughfare of the eighteenth century. The countryside around Exeter and along the estuary still appears pastoral although 160 000 now live close to it, more than all those that were living in the entire region which exported its cloth through the city in 1800.

When Payne visited Exeter it was prosperous and manufactured garments, tapestry, carpets, velvet, lace, pewter, glue, flour and beer. All the old skills required for this plus skills providing for all the normal needs of a largely self-contained community were available. The affairs of this thriving society were administered from the fourteenth-century Guildhall, which still stands in the High Street with its Elizabethan portico spanning the pavement on stone pillars.

The spirit of improvement which had started in the last quarter of the eighteenth century did not evaporate. Doubtless there were considerable slums in the city with all the filth and squalor of a medieval town. Open drains, a poor water supply, decrepit houses and inadequate sanitation must have been the lot of the very poorest. Perhaps the outbreak of smallpox in Exeter in 1777, which struck down 1850 people of whom 285 died, encouraged the progressive mood of renewal. At the same time new standards and styles of development created an imposing uniformity of Georgian terraces, and the grandeur of larger villas and country houses. For fifty years, during the last quarter of the eighteenth century and the first quarter of the nineteenth, and beyond, the towns of Devon benefited from a golden age of elegant building.

Amongst the houses in Exeter that were built around 1800 are the three-storey brick houses with sash-windows and six-panelled doors in Southernhay, which suggest an affluence and dignity of gracious town life. Nosworthy, a local builder, probably designed these and Colleton Crescent, which was built about 1805 and painted by Turner in 1828 when he stayed in the city. The Crescent stands prominently on the top of cliffs above the Quay with a fine view to the Haldon Hills, now marred slightly by the two huge gasometers built on the far side of the canal in St Thomas. Like those in Southernhay, most houses in Colleton Crescent are now used for offices because the cost of maintaining and heating them is too high for private individuals. The extravagant dignity of the eighteenth century was bought at the expense of a less egalitarian society, although the presence of servants and households they served meant that the buildings were well used.

Other early attractive terraces on Castle Hill, at Cathedral Yard and Bartholomew Street all keep the same simplicity. Rougemont Gardens, Southernhay Gardens and the Friernhay burial ground beside Bartholomew Street provide delightful spaces with mature trees which keep the spirit of elegance alive. From the burial ground one can see over the northern part of the city, and it is one of the most attractive and forgotten places in the centre of Exeter.

The Cathedral Close has several eighteenth-century buildings, and a good many more of an earlier date, overlooking a splendid green which has recently been replanted after Dutch Elm disease killed the ancient elms which grew there ten years ago. One of the interesting buildings fronting the Close is the Royal Clarence Hotel, once merely referred to as 'The Hotel'. It was originally built to provide assembly rooms for the city by William Macleworth Praed about 1768. Adjoining the original Royal Clarence, and now part of it, is

an eighteenth-century building which was formerly the Exeter Bank. During the first fifty years of the nineteenth century four of Exeter's banks were established in the Close: the Devon and Cornwall Banking Company, the City Bank and the National Provincial Bank of England, in addition to the Exeter Bank. The West of England and South Wales District Bank was in Fore Street whilst the Devon and Exeter Savings Bank was in Bedford Circus. This last bank, established in 1815, was expressly intended for the fruitful investment of savings of the 'humbler classes'. Nevertheless its location in Bedford Circus, which was one of the earliest and most stately pieces of Georgian development in the city, shows that it was as keen as its rivals to have a prestigious central site. Bedford Circus, built in 1773, was eventually destroyed by bombing during the Second World War. It was by the endeavour of local banking houses that most of the major changes, commerce and mercantile trade of this period were financed and this allowed the city to become a spacious, prosperous and attractive place in which to live.

Celia Fiennes, who visited the city at the end of the seventeenth century, would probably have recognized the vitality of the market scene a century later. She wrote:

Their market day is Friday which supplies with all things like a fair almost; the markets for meat, fowl, fish, garden things and the dairy produce takes up three whole streets, besides the large Market house set on stone pillars which runs a great length on which they lay their packs of serges, just by it is another walk within pillars which is for the yarn; the whole country is employed for at least 20 mile around in spinning, weaving, dressing, and scouring, fulling and dying of the serges, it was the most money in a week of anything in England, one week with another there is 10,000 pound paid in ready money, sometimes 15,000 pound; the weavers bring in their serges and must have their money which they employ to provide them yarn to work again; there is also a Square Court with penthouses round where the Malters are with malt, oat meal, but the serge is the chief manufacture.

Things had not changed a hundred years later and only when the two covered markets in Fore Street (Western Market, 1835/6) and Queen Street (Eastern Market, 1838) were built were the noise, good humour and smells swept from the streets to more formal surroundings, by which time the making of serges and their sale were no longer important. An echo of the earlier part of the nineteenth century still reverberates around St George's Hall, the successor to Western Market, every Friday when the number of stalls is increased. Fowler's Eastern Market has been converted into a modern shopping precinct, preserving a stately entrance.

For centuries the Cathedral had been the centre of worship for the city and surrounding region. In 1800 there were eighteen satellite churches serving the parishes of the city, plus others in St Thomas, St Leonard and Heavitree parishes, outside the city boundary. Church worship and a vigorous community spirit were often responsible for the various charitable foundations of Exeter. There were a number of Nonconformist churches and chapels, the oldest being South Street Baptist Chapel, first built in the mid-eighteenth century and rebuilt in 1822. Prejudices against Nonconformists may have remained in some cases, but the freedom of thought and religion which was leading to scientific discoveries and an insatiable desire for learning permeated society, ensuring that the Catholic Emancipation Act of 1828/9 was passed and the Test and Corporation Acts were repealed. A Roman Catholic chapel was built in Mint Lane in 1792, a Unitarian chapel was erected in 1760, and an Independent chapel in Castle Street was completed in 1796 on the site of the old county gaol. An imposing Wesleyan chapel at the Mint was built in 1812 and the activities of minorities like the Quakers continued.

For the rich, things tend to be good, but for the poor there have been varying degrees of destitution over the centuries. Without any social services, the very poor, disabled and mentally handicapped depended on the uneven charity of the well-to-do and the utilitarian provisions of the Chamber or Council that administered Exeter. It may have been the poor administration of the charitable institutions of the city, as much as the shortage of food, that led to the bread riots of 1796. Things were no better in 1801 when further bread riots took place, although on this occasion, unlike the first, the ringleader was not hung. Hand in hand with poverty went the fear of disease. Undoubtedly the limited understanding of diseases and their causes resulted in early deaths, average life expectancy being 40, although at the end of the century immunization against smallpox was being introduced.

Perhaps it was a combination of superstition, religious fervour and an ever present awareness of poverty, disease and death which allowed Joanna Southcott and others like her to extract money from the more gullible through quack medicines or extreme religious hopes. Joanna Southcott is probably the most notorious of the tricksters of this period. At the age of 50 in 1800 she declared herself a prophetess who was to give birth to the promised Shiloh, under whom her followers would enjoy a patriarchal existence on earth for a millennium. To spread the word she left for London and inspired many thousands in different parts of the kingdom who believed her to be immortal. Her followers supported her until with undisguised surprise and mortified disbelief they read in 1814 that she had died, inconsiderately failing to fulfil her optimistic promise.

Many charities administered by Exeter Corporation at the turn of the century were considered by the Parliamentary Commissioners between 1815 and 1839. In 1836 they transferred more than thirty charities to new charity trustees, at a time when an income of about £6000 should have been available to benefit all manner of needy folk. Most of those who left their money to the poor did so with particular needs in mind: for example, the £600 left by Thomas Potter in 1694 was intended to benefit eight tuckers and weavers, who could receive the annual return between them. There was the caveat that the same people could be considered only every five years, and should not be receiving parochial relief. In 1700, this was a reasonable hope but by the 1830s it was less so because there were few eligible for the charity.

Some of the institutions that were set up in the city are similarly evocative of hard times. The Society for the Relief of the Sober and Industrious Poor was established in 1799 and was in effect a coal club, since it provided coal at reduced prices subject to a puritanical expectation of the recipient leading a godly and specifically sober life. The Stranger's Friend Society visited the poor in their homes and gave monetary help. There was also a society for the relief of poor clergymen, their widows and orphans, and a Tailor's Company trust which distributed shirts and shifts to twelve poor freemen of the company, their wives or relatives.

Within the city there were 120 almshouses in which the elderly and infirm might live. Many of the almshouses or bequests seemed to be aimed at helping poor women or widows, but things were more evenly balanced with the endowment of Wynard's Hospital. This group of neat red Heavitree stone and slate buildings set around a courtyard, opposite the present West of England Eye Infirmary, drew no distinction of sex between 'twelve infirm poor people', and had a priest as warden. The buildings were probably not dissimilar to many other almshouses and are now used by various voluntary social workers, thus still helping the less able in modern society.

Just as the old and infirm were provided for, so too were the children. In different parts of the city there were schools where for small weekly payments or nothing at all several thousand children received a basic education, normally up to the age of fourteen. Many schools had been provided on a charitable basis, like the Free Grammar School in the High Street with 60 pupils and its boarding houses built nearby in 1776/7. The impetus needed to cater for a growing population and improved education is marked by the foundation in 1804 of the Ladies Charity School in Castle Street, for the improvement of 40 female poor, and in 1814 of the National Central Schools in Magdalen Street, which coped with about 230 boys and 160 girls. Shortly after, the Episcopal Charity School was rebuilt to provide for 250 scholars.

The status of the schoolmaster in charge of the Blue School, which lodged 30 boys and tutored freely 80 more, was quite high. In 1812 he received £150 per year and a further £15 each for the 30 boarders' food, lodging and clothing. With less status but perhaps a less arduous task, the schoolmistress in charge of the Blue Maids Hospital had only four girls aged 7–10 and received her lodgings, a large garden and a salary of £10 per year with a further £8 for each of the girls for board and washing. The fate of the pupils probably varied but well-brought-up girls were always needed as servants for respectable families.

A long-lasting act of charity by Dr Alured Clarke resulted in the building of the Royal Devon and Exeter Hospital in 1741. He was supported by the nobility, clergy and gentry of the city and county, and before the end of the century it was sufficiently enlarged to take 200 inpatients out of a total of 1000 being treated at any one time. The original hospital buildings in Southernhay are a monument to the compassion of society and are now being used for health administration and educational purposes, whilst the new massive grey concrete hospital on Barrack Road afflicts the eyes from most vantage points around the city. This functional building will not reach down the centuries in the same attractive way as its predecessor.

In 1801 the new lunatic asylum was built in St Thomas and preceded one at Exminster, which is only now becoming defunct as a mental hospital. A little later the Dispensary in Queen Street was established as a charity to supply the poor of the city and suburbs with medicine and surgical aid for outpatients. It was supported by charitable subscriptions just as was the Female Penitentiary that was set up with the Bishop as a patron to save the wayward souls of young ladies plucked from 'the lowest haunts of vice and degradation'. These were the continuation of a voluntary social provision which sought to provide for society, reflecting and creating the feeling of a closely knit community, with feelings of compassion, interdependent but less martialled than today's.

Exeter was the cultural centre of Devon where the wealthy rode in their carriages or in sedan-chairs to the theatre or private parties. Fashionable dress became important in an age when elegance was the aim. The French Revolution had a considerable effect on fashion, and so implicitly became more important. In the 1780s cotton and cambric became the mode, replacing satin, taffeta, silk, velvet and brocade. At this time pale colours were most popular: pale pink, ivory, lilac and pale blue.

Beau Brummell became a model for men to follow between 1794 and 1816. He was supported by the Prince Regent and so had the right connections to influence society's choice of cleanliness, rejecting the unhygienic squalor of the eighteenth century. It became smart to wear a frock-coat cut away above the waist and a velvet collar, which was cut lower than in earlier days. The cut-away tail-coat became fashionable from 1785 until the end of the century. Between 1790 and 1837 there was a gradual move away from breeches and boots to trousers, which in 1800 were of tight-fitting buckskin or corduroy. In 1820 both breeches and trousers were in vogue, although boots were fashionable for both until about 1830, when shoes and socks started to be worn with trousers.

In 1790 the tall hat with a broad brim was fashionable although by 1800 there was a lower crown, and other hats like the tricorn were common. Every well-dressed man had his hunting-crop or cane, and by 1800 nobody wore a wig, but every man could neatly tie a cravat. The fob watch was a useful asset which after 1830 was replaced by a watch and chain. Payne's men invariably wear breeches and coat whilst the woman wear bustles rather than the earlier hoops.

From 1790 women looked towards simple and dignified dress, epitomized by the introduction in 1798 of the Empire sheath, a simple gown with a high waist. The neckline was low and wide and the pastel shades complemented the simplicity. Corsets had been abandoned for a single thin petticoat and for 35 years did not return. Until the turn of the eighteenth century little underwear was worn, but following the example of Empress Josephine this changed, and it was washed as well!

During the war years it was not only the trading and economic basis of the city that was being moulded but also its defence. As in Plymouth, with the fear of invasion in 1798 and with renewed fear of Bonaparte in 1803, the defensive positions were strengthened. Already both the Cavalry Barracks on the northern side of the city and the Artillery Barracks on Topsham Road on the south side had been established. From Topsham Road it is possible to look through the imposing iron gates across the barrack square to the original buildings with a fine pediment bearing the Royal Coat of Arms, which has a lion and a unicorn with draped flags behind. Imposing and colourful, this was a daily reminder to the troops as they were drilled, and the idle onlookers watching them, of their patriotic duty. Close to the barracks along Topsham Road is a terrace of houses possibly built for the officers. A peculiarity of these Georgian buildings is their window shutters, rare features in Devon, which were provided when society was unsettled and likely to riot. The spirit of revolution was not confined to the Continent.

After 1790 the city continued to thrive with a gradual quickening of the pulse of change, affected by the war and a growing population. Amongst the things felt necessary for a civilized community were a theatre, meeting-halls and reading-rooms, all of which were present in Exeter together with several private libraries including the Devon and Exeter Institution, established in the Cathedral Close in 1813 by a number of gentlemen for the promotion of science, literature and the arts.

Amongst the earlier members of the Devon and Exeter Institution was probably the Revd John Swete, a noted diarist born in 1752 in Ashburton. He was the son of a surgeon called Nicholas Tripe but changed his name as a condition for the inheritance of a fortune from Mrs Swete, his godfather's widow. His father had inherited Oxton but did not wish to live in the house himself, so passed it to his son. It had been in the possession of Swete's mother's family, the Martyns, for centuries.

An old Etonian and a graduate of Oxford, Swete took holy orders in 1781 and was made a prebendary of Exeter in that year. He also started to rebuild Oxton in 1781 and to remodel the garden, a task which took him ten years at a cost of £6000. He recorded his efforts and described how when he first came to the property it was 'environed by garden walls – by an artificial terrace where old yews formed an avenue of pyramids, by orchards and intersecting hedges'. These he removed to leave 'a sweet valley ... gently descending between old woods of oak, through which a rivulet gurgled on, and where every object visible was not only discriminated but rural and picturesque'. Payne's picture clearly shows the remodelled house.

From Oxton John Swete could see Exeter Cathedral and the city spreading outwards from it with the pine-clad hills of Mamhead nearby. This neighbouring estate was laid out for Lord Lisburne by Capability Brown at

Oxton House

Bickham House nr Exeter

about the same time as Oxton was being remodelled. No doubt Capability Brown met and spoke with John Swete and possibly encouraged him in his intentions. Nearby, to the north and closer to the city, was Bickham House, which was also of this period and occupied by John Short. Like the lands at Oxton, the acres about Bickham were landscaped and had a view across to Kenn Church and the Exe.

Whilst travelling to North Devon, Swete recorded in his diary how he crossed the raceground and arrived at Haldon House, which was built after the style of Buckingham Palace and stood in an imposing position in its own grounds. It was the seat of Sir Robert Palk and constructed around 1730. When it came into his possession in about 1775 he set about landscaping the grounds and improving them in the same kind of fashion as neighbouring estates, planting pine and beech on the hillside around. He also built one of the most outstanding monuments in Devon, Haldon Belvedere. This is a triangular tower raised by him to honour his friend General Lawrence in 1788, and now open to the public. Inside the tower is a statue of the General and several tablets. The views from it cover much of the county and in turn it is a widely visible landmark.

These outstanding houses with their aristocratic or well-to-do owners and fashionable parkland laid out for game still relied on Exeter for their entertainment and work. Exeter was the provincial capital of Devon and the gentlemen's seats built within the folds of hills, enjoying the seclusion of forgotten valleys beside the estuary, looked towards it for their social life.

Along the estuary, outside Exeter, Topsham was the most important port to which trading vessels came, and attracted more trade than Exeter until the canal improvements of 1827. Until the nineteenth century very few vessels were unable to reach Topsham on a spring tide, and ships of between 150 and 200 tons which drew 12 feet of water could use it. Although it was a busy little port, able to depend upon an unusually good road to the city, Topsham was little more than a single irregular road running parallel to the shore. The old centre with its Dutch-gabled houses on the Quay still has the feeling of a picturesque port. The narrow streets and occasional show of cobbles, with the estuary lapping at its doorsteps and the nearby Clyst running into the Exe through flat meadows and reed-beds, capture a little of the atmosphere which has been mutilated by Topsham's recent growth and too many pylons nearby.

In 1800 the population of 2750 included mariners, lightermen, shipwrights and others whose living depended on the sea or estuary. Ships of 100 tons, too large for the canal until it was improved, called at Topsham, and many were connected with European or North American markets. The development of the private quays at Topsham at the end of the eighteenth century emphasizes its importance as a trading centre, and between 1792 and 1815 there were at least seven shipbuilders working here. In the first thirty years of the nineteenth century 92 vessels were built. Most were round-sterned lighters and ketches or square-sterned brigantines, sloops and schooners, generally under 200 tons. During the Napoleonic Wars the largest man-of-war

Mamhead

to be built was the 424 ton *Fawn* in 1807, which served in the West Indies and on the Lisbon station.

At Lympstone access from the village to the main shipping channel was through Lympstone Lake, which crossed the extensive grey mudflats. Lympstone was mainly a fishing village with cottages, a small quay and a limekiln by the water's edge. The road running inland along a valley served the mills and farms which formed the rest of the settlement. Coal, limestone, timber and naval stores were unloaded at one of its two quays. As a shipbuilding centre it was successful during the Napoleonic Wars, and between 1785 and 1833, 25 vessels were built including brigantines, sloops and cutters under 100 tons. In 1804 the *Urgent*, a 12-gunned man-of-war, was launched. After the war the trade declined and the local fishermen turned to providing London with herrings, mullet, plaice and oysters from the 100 acre oyster bed.

Since 1861 there has been a railway line running between Exeter and Exmouth, which with the considerable development in this and the latter part of the last century has affected the eastern side of the estuary. About 160 000 people are now living close to the estuary, whilst in 1800 no more than 27 000

Kenn Church

Haldon House

Starcross & Exmouth

Powderham Castle

lived in the same area. Exmouth has a population of approximately 28 000, as many as all those living in Exeter and along the estuary 180 years ago, so that the feeling of remoteness and small scale, with the dominance of the marshes, pastures and hills that overlooked it, has been lost.

The gradual change towards the role of a recreation and holiday area had begun in Exmouth with its development from around 1760 for holiday-makers and trippers from Exeter. By 1800 there were bathing-machines on the beach, moved to and fro by a rope and windlass. Until 1842, when Smeaton built the sea wall with 70 000 cubic feet of limestone, the area between Beacon Hill and the point of the estuary was a low-lying beach with sand dunes exposed to the elements. In the eighteenth century about 40 acres of the estuary were reclaimed to allow the town to grow. Since then there have been further encroachments on the estuary to provide playing-fields and car-parks, although during the past decade there has been well orchestrated and knowledgeable objection to reclaiming a further 70 acres which could reduce the feeding grounds of the Brent geese and other migrant birds. In the 1800s the white stork and kite were amongst the wildlife, which was more varied and plentiful in a remote and beautiful refuge.

The Courtenays, who owned the parish of Powderham, lived at Powderham Castle close to Starcross. Between 1750 and 1850 the Castle was substantially changed from a medieval property, although it retains much of the original building behind later façades. It is open to the public and stands in grounds which were planted extensively around 1750 when the embankment was constructed from Powderham to below Starcross. At that time ships sometimes discharged cargoes here although in the last quarter of the century silting prevented this. Some of those not employed on the estate of Lord Courtenay were able to glean a living from oysters or working in the brewery which sold its wares to the ships anchored in the Bite.

At Exmouth during the last quarter of the eighteenth century the coastal trade increased. Houses were built on Beacon Hill and there was a theatre and bowling green, with family holidays and outings to the sandy beach. Most goods for the town came via Topsham except on the spring tides. At this time a quay where the Docks are now and a slipway close by were used to land goods, including coal. In 1813, nine coasters discharged grain, stone, glass and wine at Exmouth in spite of the poor facilities, whilst colliers and larger ships discharged their loads to lighters, themselves remaining in the Bite.

Quarry at Exminster

The ferries that operated on the estuary became less important when the bridge at Countess Wear was built in 1800. At that time there were only two boatyards at Countess Wear, although between 1792 and 1812, thirteen ships were built, some of them men-of-war and East and West Indiamen. The estuary was in every way a wild and rural place and the lifeline of a large part of Devon, to which many looked for work as well as transport.

Quarry at Peamore

Exmouth to Beer

The changing coastline between Exmouth and Beer is one of the most pleasant to be found. In 1800 Exmouth had achieved a growth that has continued ever since, while Sidmouth was starting the greatest period of its expansion in the most handsome fashion, outstripping any other town during the Regency period, although Torquay was to expand even more rapidly a few years later. The sands of Exmouth were already popular and by the end of the century it was considered 'during the Summer months, an eligible retreat for the children of idleness and gaiety'. The nobility and gentry in and about Exmouth came to the town to enjoy fashionable balls at the Globe, and Lady Nelson and Lady Byron once lived in the luxurious and attractive houses of the Beacon.

High society was thriving and when courtship and marriage were fashionably romantic so too were the contrasting scandals that went with them. Lady Nelson was the subject of sympathy for the wayward behaviour of her sailor husband, who had fallen for the charms of Lady Hamilton and others. But perhaps more exciting locally were the expoits of Horatio Reeves, who in 1823 eloped with Miss Drusilla Street, a ward of court from Exeter. He was working as a chemist's assistant in Exeter at the time, and the lady was said to be worth £30 000 and only 15½ years old. It had all the ingredients for a melodramatic story with the impoverished suitor having an eye to the main chance, whilst the girl was young and innocent. In addition to the laudable excuse that Horatio wanted to get on, the girl seems to have looked older than she was. Following an injunction to prevent Reeves having any communication with the heiress and the inevitable chase to London, the pair, happy until then, were caught. It is pleasant to find that after a number of

trials and tribulations Reeves eventually married Miss Street and settled down in Exmouth.

In January 1814 the weather was so cold that the richer people in and around Exmouth contributed to help the poor. Undoubtedly the poor were by no means always deserving or genteel. Exceptionally perhaps, *Flindell's Western Luminary* reported: 'A two legged rat catcher, but perfect beast, ate, last week two raw and undrawn rats for a trifling wager at an Inn in Exmouth and would have devoured the house cat on similar terms but that the spectators had seen enough of him.'

The barbarity of some of the poorer folk was well matched by the medieval rites performed by the Church and recorded by Beatrix Cresswell. In 1805:

There was a case of open penance, which took place in Littleham Church. Susan Chamberlain of Littleham being sentenced by the Ecclesiastical Courts to walk bare foot, carrying a white wand and clothed in a white sheet from the Churchyard gate to the church, to stand through the service, and to hear sentence of excommunication read. She was allowed to keep her shoes on until she reached the church as the path was very rough. An elderly eyewitness in 1872 described her weeping bitterly and how hundreds of people from all over the County came to Littleham to see the sight.

This was not the only sight that Exmothians had enjoyed. In 1782 when the town was just a pretty neat village of cottages with no more than four or five rooms, there was a naval action between two privateers, one Dutch and the other English, the *Defiance*. For those watching from Orcombe Point there

Between Sidmouth & Exmouth – Otterton, Tor Bay, etc.

was jubilation when the English ship eventually brought the Dutchman to Exmouth as a prize. The *Defiance* had been hired as an armed ship and was probably typical of the privateers, which operated on a curious basis, similar to a private-enterprise Navy. A 'Letter of Marque' authorized these private adventurers to capture any enemy ships. In 1799 the French Government admitted that there were no French merchant ships on the high seas, partly as a result of the success of the privateers. This naturally ended their usefulness and profitability so by the early nineteenth century this type of naval activity had ended. They had often also co-operated with the Royal Navy in minor encounters where there was a chance of spoils.

Travellers between Exmouth and Lyme Regis invariably referred to the poor state of roads in East Devon, which were in fact no different from those in most other parts of the county. Traditionally the roads, little more than trackways as Payne's pictures always show, were a parish responsibility. By 1800 the parish roads were maintained by parish rates and statute labour, while toll roads were built and maintained by local trusts providing main roads for 'through traffic'. Toll keepers collected money for upkeep of the toll roads, which was not popular, and there were riots when tolls were introduced in Somerset and around Bristol. In Devon there were four miles of turnpike at Stonehouse by 1751, and from 1755 onwards there was a growing number of toll roads, first around Exeter and Plymouth. The greatest road-building activities were from 1820 onwards, and at this time the Barnstaple-to-Exeter toll road was completed by the Barnstaple Trust as far as Eggesford and by the Exeter Trust thereafter. Toll-road improvements continued until 1859 and the last were between Axminster and Honiton.

In 1830 it took eight hours to travel from Barnstaple to Taunton and thirty hours to London on the improved toll roads, although the mail coach took only five hours to Bristol and eleven hours to London. It took almost as long to reach London from Exeter, but it was an improvement on the days when the roads between London and Plymouth were described as still being 'what God left them after the flood'. That description in 1752 no doubt applied to conditions three years later, when the owners of a coach running between London and Exeter promised 'a safe and expeditious journey in a fortnight'. By the end of the century the same promise could be made for a journey lasting ten days.

The new interest in building and maintaining roads started to reduce the isolation of Devon and coincided with the improvements in road-building techniques initiated by Telford and McAdam. In 1810 McAdam was experimenting to find ways of constructing roads using different sizes of stone, intending to reduce the quagmire conditions encountered with standing water in their rutted and pitted surfaces. In 1816 he became Surveyor of Roads in the Bristol district, where his methods rapidly received popular approval so that they were adopted more generally by 1818. From the middle of the 1820s the roads became increasingly the arteries of transport, capable of competing with sea, river and canal. Over the period from 1820 to 1836, the

palmy days of coaching transformed habits and expectations and even Devon began to change. After the spread of the railway, which reached Exeter from London in 1844, and four years later reached Plymouth, there was a swift decline in roads' importance, although the carriers and carters with their horsedrawn wagons continued in strength until after the First World War.

Devon's economy in 1800 was dependent upon horses used either as pack-animals with crooks – a wooden framework to support panniers – or less frequently to pull carts. They were often ridden with the wife as a pillion passenger. Coaches brought prosperity to the county with coachmen, guards, horse-keepers and ostlers all employed to serve intrepid travellers. In some parts of the county there was the added hazard of highwaymen, who unkindly held up coaches as they slowly struggled uphill on unimproved roads. Even with the improvement of roads the average working life of a horse in the 1830s was no more than four years, and many coach horses 'died in harness' through the roughness of roads and consequent strain of being driven to the limit.

In Devon the state of the roads, or rather rough tracks, varied according to the type of soil over which they passed. Riding on the clays of Devon was almost impossible even on horseback in winter, and entirely impossible in a carriage or on a cart, whose wheels often rubbed the sides of narrow sunken ways. Tracks meandered cross-country, avoiding quagmires and ownership boundaries alike, and their dismal state effectively helped isolate the dozens of small inland hamlets and villages for four or five months of the year.

These conditions helped to sustain ignorance and superstition. The candle and lantern were the lights of winter, when ghosts, goblins, wraiths and other spirits were discussed in the same terms as Christian beliefs. Faith in witches and spells and other superstitions was as real in towns as in isolated villages. The invention of gas lighting by Frederic Winsor in 1804, used for lighting streets, helped to dispel evil spirits as well as the equally violent thieves or murderers so at home in the dark. In 1817 Exeter was the first town in Devon to be lit by gas, and during the next twenty years most towns benefited similarly. Today the view from Haldon Hill of Exeter and the street-lighting connecting it with Exmouth is an impressive sight and a picturesque attraction of modern technology.

Payne's paintings of the coast east of Exmouth do not show the great variety of cliffs and landscape although they do show its remoteness. From the cliffs at Sidmouth it is possible to see most of Lyme Bay. The 500 foot red sandstone cliffs are not unlike those of Dawlish, and at Sandy Bay to the west Straight Point has its own stacks of red rock rising from the sea inhabited only by gulls and cormorants. To the east are the white chalk cliffs around Branscombe and Beer. If the artist had visited this area fifty years later he would have been astonished at the change, although he could have seen the initial results of the first of several landslides between Branscombe and Lyme Regis. In March 1790 about 10 acres of clifftop land called Southdown slipped about 250 feet and created the broken landscape of the chalk undercliff, full of pinnacles and gulfs, now a nature reserve and dramatic route for the coastal path. The tangled undergrowth on either side is the home of robins, blackbirds, yellowhammers and linnets, whilst crows and seagulls soar about the magnificent cliffs. After 150 years mature beech and oak have colonized the broken ground and thick vines festoon trees like a tropical forest.

Budleigh Salterton was described in the late eighteenth century as nothing but a small collection of fishermen's cottages and sheds, and this is accurately implied in Payne's painting. There was no marine parade along the front, only the River Otter soaking through the pebble ridge to the sea. Between 1790 and 1815 Budleigh gradually became popular with visitors in the summer season, and by 1850 it was a fashionable seaside resort. The main street, which passes beside a pleasant stream to the sea front, was gradually developed during these years with an inn and shops, and some fine Regency and early-Victorian houses were constructed on the slopes above it. Holy Trinity Church was built by Lord Rolle in 1812/13, and was extended in 1837 for the increased population. At about the same time, in 1811, a Wesleyan chapel was built and continued to be used until replaced in 1904.

By 1820 Budleigh Salterton was developing rapidly although mackerel were still caught close to the pebble bar. Later there was a national school, two circulating libraries and a reading-room. Today Budleigh is an attractive town whose large number of retired inhabitants can enjoy the pebbly beach with boats pulled up on it and walks along the River Otter, where heron, kingfishers and dippers fly, beyond Otterton to Ottery St Mary.

Otterton, about 1½ miles along the river, is one of the most attractive villages in East Devon, with pleasant Elizabethan farmhouses and cottages. The Green has a row of cob-and-thatch cottages, and whether the main street is viewed up towards the top of Fore Street or back down towards the Craft Centre in the old Victorian mill buildings, it is appealing. There was once a priory next to the Church of St Michael, which was rebuilt except for the tower in 1879 and stands on high land overlooking the old three-span stone bridge. In 1800, although Otterton was not growing it had its own schoolmaster and all the trades needed to sustain its community: bakers, blacksmiths, carpenters, butchers and a draper, supported by the prosperous farming community.

Between Otterton and East Budleigh is Bicton House, the home of Lord Rolle, who at the end of the eighteenth century rebuilt the old house to create a substantial brick mansion. He removed the old Elizabethan gardens and replanted in the fashionable informal style adopted by Capability Brown and Repton, with a pinetum and a fine lake. The gardens are now open to the public, whilst the mansion is used for Bicton College of Agriculture. Even in 1800 the fine beech trees were a feature and the approach to the College along an avenue of monkey-puzzle trees must be a unique Victorian quirk. It was not until 1850 that the new Church of St Mary replaced the old one, Holy Trinity, which in 1800 stood encircled by trees in the lower part of the park. It was intended to take it down when the new church was completed, but the ancient

tower of Holy Trinity is visible from the Newton Poppleford road and has recently been repaired.

East Budleigh is a neat village of white-painted cob-and-thatch houses lining a narrow street that ascends to the largely fifteenth-century red sandstone Church of All Saints. The cobbled edges of the street close to the church attractively complement the old houses, which were ancient in Payne's day. The village used to be divided into higher, middle and lower parts, but with a school and modern properties it has become a single large village which, like Otterton and Budleigh Salterton, has a pleasant brook running through part of it. Although East Budleigh has grown since the last century, especially with bungalow estates, the view from the churchyard leaves an impression of a hardly changing scene. Sir Walter Raleigh was born at a farmhouse called Hayes Barton in 1552, and the family pew with its crest and date 1537 is amongst some beautifully carved bench-ends in the church. The old thatched farmhouse, owned by the National Trust, has projecting wings and a central porch like other Elizabethan buildings and lies a little way from the village amidst rolling countryside.

A further two miles north on the River Otter, Newton Poppleford's population of around 500 remained static. Only since the Second World War, with increased commuting to Exeter, has it grown appreciably. In 1800 there was a chapel of ease, St Mark's, replaced by the Church of St Luke in 1897. Two hundred years ago the village stretched along the Exeter-to-Sidmouth road on the west side of the Otter, which could be forded here. The oldest cob-and-thatch houses, probably dating from the early sixteenth century, stand near the river, although old buildings are scattered along the length of the village, with the newer estates behind. Two cattle fairs were held here each year and until recently it was mainly a farming community. So too was Tipton St John, to the north, with several fine old cob-and-thatch houses.

Ottery St Mary, further up river, was a growing market-town of 2400 at the turn of the eighteenth century, and about 1540 were employed in farming. The lord of the manor had enclosed extensive common land and planted trees around this thriving town. Two annual cattle markets and two cattle fairs were held in Ottery, which was surrounded by prosperous farmland whose hedgerows had many fine beeches and elms. The Church of St Mary is one of the largest in the county and was modelled on Exeter Cathedral. Close to it are attractive houses and shops, some of which were old in 1800 while others were built around this time. Most have Georgian façades. A plaque on the churchyard wall commemorates the poet Samuel Coleridge, who was born at the family home next to the church in 1775.

A new woollen-mill was opened at the end of the eighteenth century, built of red brick and slate on Mill Street close to the river. There is a tumbling weir which was used to power the machinery and a pleasant walk along the mill leat. Close by Mill Street were some ancient houses, one of which had been occupied by Sir Walter Raleigh, but by 1794 they were in a dilapidated condition. In 1805 they were burnt down and a handsome new brick house

Budleigh Salterton

Sidmouth

took their place; this is now used for an old persons' home. Ottery was a neat and well-paved town although age had contrived to give its buildings an uneven appearance. It still has its mill, now used for making electrical goods, and a curving street to the town square. The terraces of the older roads that meet here are neat but any elegance is limited to the area around the church and the Jubilee Memorial below it.

In 1810 the lord of the manor for Ottery St Mary was M. Howe Esq. and he was responsible for holding the court leet and court baron. These were held yearly and appointed an inspector of weights and measures, a water bailiff, an ale taster, a scavenger and other officers. The privileges of the lords of the manor and their jurisdiction stemmed from 1189, when all of the manors were in existence. They varied in size, the way they held courts and the punishments given, but the general isolation of towns and villages made them necessary. Their value to the community diminished as time went by, but until Tudor times and the appointment of Justices of the Peace, these courts held in the local manor-house, often just a large farmhouse, dealt with the problems of society. Some statutes recognized the jurisdiction of both Justices and the manorial courts, like that of 1607 on drunkenness. It was not until the Municipal Corporations Act of 1835 that the court leet was stripped of its powers to dispense justice. The system of Justices, the inability to deal with highways and bridges, the enclosure of common land and the decline of copyholders all reduced the ancient medieval powers embodied in the manors.

Enclosure of commons by agreement in the seventeenth century, by private acts in the eighteenth and by the General Enclosures Act after 1836 did away with the need to regulate cropping and common pasture practices, which had been an important part of manorial-court work. Copyholders held land on a permanent and hereditary basis from the lord of the manor, who owned the freehold. After the seventeenth century it was not legal to increase the number of copyholders and over the centuries most land held from the manor was converted by agreement to leasehold or freehold. The remnants of this system were eventually abolished by the Law of Property Act 1922. The development of toll roads and accessibility further reduced the power of the manorial courts, which no longer held the jurisdiction for a multitude of 'islands' within the countryside.

Between the Otter and the River Sid lies a band of rich arable land criss-crossed by narrow high-banked Devon lanes. The descent from Peak Hill to Sidmouth gives the modern traveller a sight of the whole town, which has a population of about 12 600, spreading back from the most ancient part around Sidmouth Church to Sidford. Even though Sidmouth was starting to become the most popular resort in Devon, in 1800 the town was only a fraction of its present size with a population of 1250. Already the imposing Fortfield Terrace was being built and it was one of the 'gayest' places in Devon, where one might stroll along the front, buy ice-cream or play billiards at the Shed. This was built close to the esplanade, with the ground floor open whilst the upper rooms were supported on columns and used for playing cards and other games.

Sidmouth was a pretty market-town where there were a good number of fishermen. Its popularity as a resort grew at this time and with it the population of not only notables but their servants and shopkeepers too. The London Inn was the most important hostelry in the town, where a ball was held every Wednesday and where there were assembly rooms. There was a theatre, two circulating libraries as well as bathing-machines. The present Church of St Nicholas has taken the place of a much older one which was altered and added to in 1822 but completely rebuilt except for the tower in 1859/60. The Old Presbyterian Meeting House built in Upper High Street in 1770 was the oldest Nonconformist church, and only in 1837 did the Wesleyans build their chapel. The town had several charities which helped the poor at the turn of the eighteenth century.

The war did not entirely pass Sidmouth by, and a fort with four guns stood close to where the cricket club plays today. After the war the fort was dismantled and for some time two of the cannons were placed on end in the tower of the parish church to support the belfry floor. There was also a corps of Sea Fencibles raised in Sidmouth, and at Peak Hill a signal station was established, one of a series along the coast of Devon which used a system of telegraphs and beacons and were intended to warn of any enemy invasion. General Simcoe, who between 1791 and 1796 was the first lieutenant-governor of Upper America, today's Ontario, and who lived at Wolford near Honiton, had voluntary troops encamped on Woodbury Hill, to complete the martial feeling.

Between 1790 and 1830 many of the most-attractive Regency terraces and villas were built. Invariably they were stucco fronted, sometimes with Georgian sash-windows and handsome six-panelled doors with fine brass doorknockers, at other times adopting the more romantic Gothic style. Knowle Cottage, built by Lord le Dispenser in 1816, like many other 'cottages' was a substantial mansion, although thatched to suit the romantic feeling of the time. Today owners have frequently painted their properties white or some pastel shade and kept them attractive. Elysian Fields, a row of magnificent detached buildings set in beautifully mature gardens, could have been built only at a time of elegance and inequality, whilst Lord Gwydir bought the manor with Old Hayes, on a site that had been occupied from time immemorial, and demolished it to make way for his grand romantic cottage, now the Woodlands Hotel.

The Woolbrook Glen Hotel, like the Woodlands Hotel, is one of several superior hotels which were once fine private houses. Sidmouth had reached such a height of elegance and popularity that the Duke of Kent, who had stopped at Woolbrook Glen in October 1819 whilst looking for a house for himself and his family, returned again in December. This time he brought the Duchess and infant Princess Victoria. It was an eventful visit. First some small boys shooting guns at birds nearby shattered a window of the room where

Princess Victoria was asleep. Shortly after the Duke of Kent died, having walked in the snow, got his feet wet and not changed his boots. When visited by the local barber Mr Turner, who shaved him with some difficulty because he had a sort of spasmodic hiccups, he was being attended by two London physicians as well as a local surgeon. This suggests that the local diagnosis owes more to mothers giving warnings to their children than to wet feet really having caused his death.

The Duke of Kent's death might not have been a good advertisement for the healthy and invigorating qualities of the town, but the great storm of 22 November 1824 might have been worse. The waves broke through the bank of earth that acted as protection from the sea and as a walk along the front and flooded much of the town. There was little check to the town's growth, and in 1837/8 to avoid another disastrous flood and provide a new walk, the modern esplanade was built using substantial blocks of stone. Before this time, in 1831, the Grand Duchess Helene of Russia stayed at No. 8 Fortfield Terrace for three months accompanied by a retinue of about a hundred servants, who were put up in various houses throughout the town. Her visit is commemorated by the double-headed eagle in the pediment of the terrace.

The project to build a harbour at Sidmouth put forward in 1811 was never implemented because of disputes about the best place to construct it, although after Acts of Parliament in 1825 and 1836, £12000 worth of preliminary work was undertaken. Fortunately the sea was left to the fishermen, who at Sidmouth caught some of their fish by using poles with nets stretched across them so that the fall of the tide left fish stranded there. The east side of the town, not far from the River Sid, was an area of poorer dwellings known as the Marsh, and up river from the beach there was a rough boggy stretch with houses continuing up the valley. Today the Hams is an attractive stretch of parkland taking the place of this earlier wilderness and reaching up to Sidford. In 1800 Sidford was a small village with nothing more than some ancient cottages and a narrow pack-horse bridge across the Sid, which has been incorporated into the modern bridge. The old cottages at Sidford on the Honiton Road are probably 400 years old and now part of a large village.

Beyond Sidford is Sidbury, a marvellous compact village with a number of good houses and ancient terraces around the parish church. Until 1801 the Dean and Chapter of Exeter Cathedral held the manor but then sold it to William Guppy and other freeholders. It later came into the hands of the Hunt family, who lived at Court Hall, the manor-house. Another fine house nearby is Sand, which is opened to the public and has been in the ownership of the Huyshe family for centuries. Modern development has increased the size of the village, which in 1800, taken with Sidford and the farms within the parish, had 1200 inhabitants but took another fifty years to grow by 600.

The stretch of coast to Beer is the traditional area for smuggling, although in reality smugglers enjoyed the benefit of long coastlines to the north and south of the county and a choice of 1500 rates of customs duty to avoid. The men of the little stone and thatched villages of Branscombe and Salcombe Regis would have been as active in smuggling as they were in farming and fishing. Both these communities have grown but the older buildings and farms clearly show their extent in 1800. They have an air of remote tranquillity and are pleasant places to visit. At the higher part of Branscombe, the village bakery of Collier and Son stands amongst two or three old thatched properties and still uses faggots for firing the ovens, which was the general way of doing things two centuries ago. The long low pile of brushwood bundles is a rare sight now, and it is made the more pleasing by a working smithy trading nearby.

John Rattenbury, born in 1778, was amongst the most notorious smugglers along this part of the coast. His memoirs were published in 1837 and included a good commentary on his times, although it is likely his tales of smuggling and an adventurous life may have been exaggerated. He started his smuggling out of Lyme in 1794 and found it considerably less boring than fishing, which occupied most people in his own village of Beer. Like others he was impressed into the Navy and was sent on board the *Royal William* at Spithead, but escaped. There was a press-gang based at Lyme which he had to avoid, and he similarly had to dodge the naval personnel sent from Portsmouth to catch him. Anyone arresting a deserter was given a reward and the deserter was punished by flogging.

In 1800 he signed on a brig at Topsham which needed hands. This was engaged in the Newfoundland trade, but on their way from Newfoundland with fish to Oporto, a Spanish privateer captured them at Vigo. Rattenbury managed to escape and in 1801 joined Captain Drummond on the *Alert*, an English privateer, but after a fruitless expedition returned to smuggling. Later, in 1805, he joined a privateer from Weymouth, again failed to enjoy captured booty and swore never to try his hand on a privateer in future.

Amongst his adventures was one in 1806 when the *Duke of York*, a customs cutter, caught him and his colleagues in the midst of smuggling kegs of gin. They had sunk most of the kegs when they were arrested and the captain of the cutter offered to release them if they agreed to bring up the rest. Having done so, they were indignant when the customs men went back on their word and took them into Dartmouth for trial. As they passed Dartmouth Castle Rattenbury dived over the side and once again escaped ashore, and would have got away had not two elderly women betrayed his hiding-place. With an escort from the cutter strengthened by constables from the town, the smugglers were taken to the town hall, where the magistrate gave them the option to pay a £100 fine each, to go on board a man-of-war, or to go to gaol. After a short while in prison, the conditions were so bad they agreed to go on board a man-of-war, hoping to escape. They were eventually placed on the brig *Safeguard*, although with his smooth tongue Rattenbury managed to return to the customs cutter, from which he escaped and got a fisherman to row him to Kingswear. He gave the man £1 for his trouble and avoided the marines and sailors who were sent after him, going on foot to Brixham.

Beer nr Sidmouth

Seaton, looking eastward

Rattenbury returned to smuggling near his home at Beer, which had a single road running down to the beach, unlike the town of today, which has spread up the hillside. The water conduits which run down the side of the main street are probably not unlike those of earlier years. Some houses use stone from the nearby quarries, which have been productive since Roman times. Some of the underground workings have recently been opened to the public and graffiti from about 1800 are a point of interest. These workings are on the south side of a narrow road that runs past the more modern quarries opposite, from which stone is being taken to repair Exeter Cathedral.

Both Beer and Seaton held pleasure fairs once a year and the Church of St Gregory at Seaton served both communities, although Beer had a chapel of ease as well as an Independent chapel. Like other towns on the coast, both grew during the first thirty years of the nineteenth century but Seaton also expanded very swiftly later, after the coming of the railway. Seaton has become a rather brash holiday resort in recent years, however the marshes that stretch back along the River Axe probably keep faith with earlier times. The town has the disadvantage of electricity cables and intrusive buildings and car-parks along the front, but the marsh flowers, birds and butterflies have not changed, and curiously the tramway that passes through the marshland up to Colyford just adds to its interest as well as satisfying holiday-makers. Birds of prey hunt for small mice or rabbits, or fish in the river. The curlew with its distinctive cry, lapwings and oyster-catchers haunt the mudflats when the tide is out, and gulls wheel above the boats moored on the estuary. The bridge that crosses the river close to the beach is the oldest concrete bridge in the country and is likely to be supplemented by another further up the river, intruding still further on this attractive spot.

Seen across the marshes, Axmouth with its church tower might have stood still for two centuries, although when it is visited it soon becomes clear that there are modern buildings as well as some good stone Elizabethan houses. The people of Axmouth, like those of Beer and Seaton, were engaged mainly in farming and fishing although some were employed in salt making. Colyford, on the main coast road, was little more than a number of run-down cottages. Contrasting with this, Stedcombe House, an imposing building constructed in 1694, still stands in its own attractive parkland looking across the marshes to the sea.

Colyton, to the north by the Umborne, a tributary of the Axe, was a substantial little market-town which had a fine church, St Andrew's, with an octagonal bell tower. It thrived on the wool industry until the nineteenth century and grew by 1000 over the fifty years from 1800 to about 2600. Close to the church are the oldest buildings, mostly modernized in Victorian times, which disguises their Tudor origins. Inside, coffered ceilings with moulded beams, or Elizabethan panels and plasterwork ceilings show their true age. Buildings round the square and along the narrow roads nearby are often of stone, rendered and painted white with thatch or slate roofs. Stone walls along the footpaths and a quietness, in spite of cars looking for a parking space, help create an outstanding small town, sheltered on three sides by rolling hills.

Whilst the woollen industry languished there was work in the paper-mill, tannery, brewery, foundry and corn-mills. In 1800 Colyton had a Unitarian chapel and in 1814 an Independent chapel was built, while later a Wesleyan chapel served the growing community. Like other towns it had lands which were held in trust, the feoffees being 'twenty men of Colyton'. Money from the land and nine houses held by them was used to bring water to the town, distributed to the poor and £30 per year paid to the master of the free school for teaching twenty boys to read, write and do arithmetic. The schoolroom stands in the square next to the churchyard, and was built in 1612. With its beer houses, post office and carters, Colyton was a thriving town although lacking the tourist interest which attracted Payne.

In addition to the farmers and fishermen at Beer, there was also a thriving lace-making business. Outworkers in their cottages made delicate, intricate lace which later became called Honiton Lace, although widely produced in East Devon. At the turn of the eighteenth century about 2500 people were employed in Honiton and the surrounding villages making lace called Honiton Point Lace, and sometimes bone or thread lace. It sold for between one shilling and one guinea a yard and the best was made from finest Antwerp thread. The prosperity from this skill was checked after 1815 by the manufacture of net lace at Tiverton.

In 1815 a large woollen-mill which had been built in 1790 at Tiverton was purchased by Messrs Heathcote and Company, who added to it and converted it to a lace works where a bobbin net machine powered by a water-wheel made a cheaper product. Although it checked the traditional lace industry elsewhere, this mill provided some employment for those who had previously worked in the declining woollen-mills in the town. Tiverton was a substantial town of 6500 in 1800 which was growing rapidly, and with the building of the Grand Western Canal in 1810 looked set for continuing prosperity. Like Honiton, it remained a prosperous market-town, but neither recaptured their relative industrial importance of earlier times, although both had been affected by industrialization and the changes that resulted.

Shaugh Bridge

Around Dartmoor

In 1794 Robert Fraser drew up a report about agriculture in Devon for the Board of Agriculture and Internal Improvement. He discovered that because the size of the county was so great it was very rare to find a man acquainted with any part of the county except his own and that practices varied in different parts. Payne's pictures rarely show farming scenes but they are sometimes included in romantic or dramatic scenery.

At the end of the eighteenth century farmland was often occupied for a period of 99 years, determinable on three lives, and these farms were regarded as the estate of the holder, like a freehold. Some of this land was let out to subtenants, but some was held for life and passed on. Farmers might have two or three holdings, which rarely exceeded 40 acres. Very few farmers held more than 200 acres. There were several families who owned substantial tracts of countryside but most estates were relatively small, allowing a good number of gentlemen to live comfortably on their estates. They had their own social circle and lived on good terms with 'the respectable yeomanry' of the neighbourhood. In the South Hams, Fraser noted that the yeomanry looked after their dependants with consideration and care, and provided for the poor. There were a variety of leases and the shorter ones which did not provide the kind of security to encourage investment to maintain the quality of the farm were condemned.

Some labourers lived in cottages which were part of the holding or 'lived in'. They worked from six in the morning until six at night during the summer and from seven until five in the winter with arrangements for the Sabbath. Part of their wages was normally provided as cider, something that by 1820 was beginning to be decried because of its effects on the labourers and their

families. In 1800 a labourer could expect a shilling a day and a quart of cider. Threshing, ploughing and cutting, setting and steeping hedges were all paid for on a piecework basis. Hedging and making up the wood into faggots earned four to ten pence per yard and the building of walls on Dartmoor six pence per yard.

However popular the cider was with the labourer, who at harvest-time was given as much as he wanted, the cider tax of 1763 reduced its profitability for the farmer, so a good number of orchards were cut down and the decline in their renewal reduced the yield. The copyholder traditionally had an orchard and in some seasons he was able to pay the lord of the manor's rent from it. Cider was produced in most parts of the county, with particular success in the neighbourhood of Exeter, Chudleigh, Newton Abbot, Paignton and Totnes. The cider was popular in London as well as locally because of its quality, and the parish of Staverton's sweet cider was renowned. Cider sold for between 18 and 25 shillings per hogshead and in 1794 a Chudleigh farmer made 80 hogshead (320 gallons) from three acres and received a guinea per hogshead.

Cider making had followed the traditional method in which the apples were pulped in a granite trough by rolling a granite wheel over them, then made into a 'cheese' and pressed. The 'cheese' consisted of layers of crushed apples piled on top of each other and held in by layers of straw folded over at the ends like a series of envelopes. The heavy wooden presses on wooden or metal screws were gradually forced down and juice collected and put into vats to ferment before being transferred into barrels. By 1800 machines were taking the place of the stone crushing-mills, but the technique remained the same. Several varieties of apple were popular including the 'red streaked'. These might have been similar to Tom Putts, a variety of cider apple developed by a barrister, Thomas Putt, who lived at Gittisham from 1722 to 1787. Tom Putt apples can be used for cooking, eating or cider making, and are a fine crimson.

An interest in improving the quality of crops as well as the yield led to the founding of the Devonshire Agricultural Society in 1791 and the formation of branches in every part of the county over the next fifty years. It was also part of their intention to improve the lot of the agricultural workers, although there was little distinction between them and the smallholders with a few acres. Turnips were introduced into a crop rotation and often sown after ploughing up rough grass, skirting and beat burning, which involved raking together the dried grasses and roots some time after ploughing before burning them. A crop of barley might be sown after turnips had been fed to cattle around February, followed by wheat the next year and then barley followed by grass. Drilling in seed rather than broadcasting had been tried by Mr Byne of Stockledge near Chudleigh and a farmer on the Templer estate at Stover in 1794.

Other important changes came from the needs of war. Up to the turn of the century either two or four oxen were used for ploughing, generally with a pair of horses leading. The demand by the Navy for beef, whether or not it was tender, reduced the use of oxen and increased the use of horses. This change was substantially adopted and by 1850 the use of oxen was sufficiently rare for the practice to be remarked upon as 'still' occurring. Carts were rarely used before 1800, and when they were, oxen or horses pulled them, but after the war carts and wagons drawn by horses were widely introduced, together with the two-horse plough.

Amongst the most notable of those introducing new animal breeds and techniques was Sir Francis Buller, who purchased the Prince Hall estate. Sir Francis had been born at Downes, a fine imposing property just outside Crediton, on 17 March 1746. He was educated at Ottery St Mary grammar-school, and whilst there lived at the home of Samuel Coleridge's father, later obtaining a presentation to the Bluecoat School in London for the poet. Buller became the youngest man to be appointed a judge in England when on the 6 May 1778 at the age of 32 he became a judge of the King's Bench, on the recommendation of Lord Mansfield.

He was a small but handsome man with a commanding forehead and piercing eye, given to playing cards. Towards the end of his career, in which he was noted for a keen legal brain and sometimes hasty and biased judgements, Lord Mansfield, whom Buller served well during the last two years of Mansfield's life, attempted to get him promoted. The Government hesitated and wavered. Pitt apparently recalled a trial at Bodmin, affecting some political rights relating to a rotten borough owned by the Buller family, at which Buller had presided and shown a not impartial attitude to benefit his family. Lord Thurlow stated that Pitt 'hesitated long between the corruption of Buller and the intemperance of Kenyon'. A comfort for being passed over was that Buller became a baronet on 13 January 1790. He continued as a judge for a further ten years until he died in June 1800.

He helped introduce many innovations on Dartmoor including importing Scottish black cattle, which did sufficiently well for him to sell at £7 or £8 per head. The Dartmoor sheep provided tasty mutton which was in great demand, but Buller experimented by introducing some South Down sheep. He had less fortune when he planted 40 000 larch and other conifers close to Prince Hall. These failed although another plantation close to Two Bridges at Bear Down Farm thrived, and its successor can be seen from the Tavistock road. Buller did not stick at farming improvements but also built a small inn at Two Bridges, which has grown over the years, and also introduced a local pleasure fair there.

The moor provided a background for some of Payne's pictures, but it was always regarded as a hostile place and only at the end of the eighteenth century had a good road across it. The mists and snows were inhospitable, although some, like Sir Francis Buller, endeavoured to harness the 'wilderness' for agriculture. Around the edge of the high bleak open moor in the eighteenth century were unenclosed areas suitable for planting trees and rearing sheep or cattle. In 1793 between 110 000 and 120 000 sheep summered on open land but enclosures were probably responsible for a decline to 80 000 four years later, and to 60 000 by 1810, although the less hardy breeds introduced might also have been responsible. Many thousands of acres were enclosed between 1790 and 1850 and helped to create much of the attractive countryside that fringes the moor, leaving 60 000 acres of central Dartmoor a picturesque but untamed place. For those living in the south of the county during the Napoleonic Wars, plans were made to go to Dartmoor if there was an invasion, taking as large a stock of salt bacon for sustenance as possible. The fear of the French was great enough to overcome the disadvantages of Dartmoor's inhospitable climate.

Bickleigh Valley stretches south from Shaugh Moor, where vast china-clay workings have taken the place of much smaller ones which made little impact on the landscape in 1800, to Marsh Mills on the River Plym. It was a well-known beauty spot although there was considerable industrial activity. The bridge at Shaugh Prior is a little way from the village, which in 1790 was little more than a few poor cottages around the impressive Church of St Edward, King and Martyr with its distinctive tower.

The Plym and Meavy meet above Shaugh Bridge, where the oaks on land owned by the National Trust are festooned with lichen. The beauty of this valley through which the combined torrents of the rivers tumble has changed but must be similar to that of the eighteenth century. From the old stone bridge it is easy to walk beside the banks of the Plym through mature woods, which sometimes open into fields where ponies graze, to Bickleigh Bridge. The gently rising valley sides steepen to the east, trout and salmon swim in the Plym and dippers flit about the gurgling torrent. Bickleigh has grown and

Bickley from Shaugh Bridge

is dominated by the buildings of the Royal Marines, but below the bridge the valley narrows slightly before widening out above Plym Bridge.

Plym Bridge is still a beauty spot and walkers can enjoy the ancient oak, alder and ash. The old railway is now a cycle track and footpath passing up the valley past the impressive Cann Quarries, where clearance work has revealed old quarry buildings and tumbledown houses. The size of the quarry face, from which tons of stone were taken for roof slates or walls, is impressive. The Dartmoor Railway – a granite tramway similar to that from Haytor – was built in 1819 and passes through the eastern part of the valley. It was used to carry stone from the moor and the opening of these granite quarries helped to provide employment when the Prison at Princetown closed in 1816. Paintings of the valley embody the same natural features seen today, although the coniferous plantations of Cann Wood, Great Shaugh, Trill Wood and Squares Wood are extensive and less pleasing than the hardwoods that preceded them. On the upper parts of Dartmoor the greatest changes since 1800 have been the planting of conifers.

To the south-west of the moor, close to the source of the Plym and about seven miles from Tavistock, lies Meavy. With its ancient granite church and equally old oak renowned in Victorian times, hollow, leaning and propped up, it is probably as typical a small moorland village as any. In 1800 about 240 parishioners lived mainly in a scattering of houses grouped close to the Church of St Peter. Meavy grew slowly in the first half of the nineteenth century and a little more later, whilst the attractive small village of Sheepstor with a population of 100 grew hardly at all. Sheepstor, in the picturesque valley of the Meavy, is close to the open moorland, beneath Sheep's Tor, and had two large rabbit warrens. The keeping of rabbits was not uncommon and the Warren House Inn near Moretonhampstead commemorates a warren nearby, which at the end of the eighteenth century had no wall to keep the roaming rabbits in. The fourteenth-century church at Sheepstor is interesting as much for its carved bench-ends as for the graves of the Brookes of Sarawak, in particular James Brooke, who was born in Bengal in 1803, became Rajah of Sarawak in 1841, retired to Burrator in the parish in 1863, and died in 1868.

Close to Sheepstor on Yellowmead Down, where buzzards soar, are hut circles, and these like others on the moor were a constant source of speculation for amateur archaeologists as they are today. The locals had their own superstitions and beliefs whilst the better educated took a lively academic interest in them. Nearby along the granite-walled road is Burrator Reservoir, which was constructed in 1891 and later enlarged. It is a feature which, although obtrusive and not entirely in character with the moor, like the more modern reservoir at Meldon, is still attractive and a grand place to walk.

North of Sheepstor is Horrabridge, which at this time was no more than a scatter of houses, although the bridge and much of its beauty have been kept to the present day.

Mavey & Sheep's Torr, Dartmoor

To the north along the edge of Dartmoor, which stretches on in rolling hills, is Brentor, often hidden in the winter drizzle and mist, with St Michael's Church on the top of it. The scene has hardly changed since Payne's day. In autumnal gloom the clouds are often well below the summit of this 1130 foot knoll. A church has stood here and been used as a landmark from Plymouth since the twelfth century. It has been renovated from time to time and was substantially restored in 1889.

From Brentor it is possible to see the remains of Lydford Castle, which stand on a mound close to the little Church of St Petrox. In 1080 Lydford was taxed on a par with London and was the centre for tin taken from the moor. The Stannary Court was held in the castle and rough justice meted out to those brought before it accused of mining offences. By 1800 the castle was as dilapidated as it is today although the large stone tower was said to be out of repair rather than in ruins. A mile and a half away are the impressive Lydford Falls, in a well-wooded and picturesque gorge which is now owned by the National Trust.

Gilpin tells the story of a man coming from London and making haste on his journey through a wet and windy night. He seems to have been unfamiliar

Harrow Bridge

Brent Torr

Lidford

seats, etc., cut in rough stone, were almost complete although the courts had long been outmoded. The 'Stannary Parliaments', originally held in the open air at Crockern Tor, were later held at one of the Stannary Towns. These were Ashburton, Chagford, Plympton and Tavistock, where tin was weighed and stamped.

The Castle Inn, next to the remains of Lydford Castle, offers a more cheerful welcome and like many of the older properties in the scattered village is built of dark stone and slate. At Bridestowe nearby the use of granite and other local stone marks the older buildings, and both villages are set in beautiful and remote countryside. Close to Bridestowe is Burley Wood, the site of a prehistoric castle. Along the A30 towards Okehampton, the wild countryside and steep untamed slopes of the moor on one side, and a seemingly endless series of ridges and isolated farms on the other echo the empty lands of Devon 200 years ago.

At Okehampton the romantic remains of the castle stand on a mound within a valley through which the River Okement flows. In 1800 they were invariably described as hung with ivy and surrounded by fine oak woodland, which at about this time was being cleared, probably for the Navy or at least to benefit from the higher wartime prices. Until the castle, which was the home of the Courtenays, the Earls of Devon, and their retinues, was dismantled in 1539, the town had considerable prestige. It was a pocket borough and sent two members to Parliament up to 1832, although it still remained a borough until 1974. The park which surrounded the castle included about 1600 acres along the southern side of the West Okement Valley. Today there is a car-park for visitors, the castle grounds are fenced and visitors charged to walk round the ruins, no longer mouldering, apparently about to collapse and hidden beneath festoons of ivy, but neat and repointed, well maintained and approached by a path surrounded by grass trimmed to satisfy tidy minds. The encouragement of many more visitors has been at the expense of wildness and the romantic scene.

The Courtenays had given 300 acres of land for use by townspeople as a common, but the lord of the manor in 1800 or thereabouts claimed the summer use of the land for himself leaving others to use it in the winter. By 1850 it was being enclosed, and 85% of it went to the lord of the manor.

Okehampton was a thriving market-town and at the turn of the eighteenth century 1400 lived in the parish, slowly growing by 50% to about 2100 in 1850. A market was held in the Shambles every Saturday, and farm produce was taken to both Exeter and Plymouth from here. In 1826 a new large market hall was built to remove the inconvenience caused by the street trading. Within the past few years this has been refurbished and shops have been built behind those on the main street. On the Saturday before Christmas a large market was held in the town and on the one after a 'giglet' or pleasure fair took place. This type of event might well have included cock-fights and bull-baiting as part of the common fun of the fair.

The cattle brought to market would normally have been Devons, which

with the country and should have crossed the gorge by a short, narrow wooden bridge. Using whip and spurs he eventually arrived at his destination and read the next morning how the bridge had collapsed in the storm, and only then recalled how his horse had at one stage in his furious gallop given a mighty bound, which he then realized had been to cross this narrow chasm and the water tumbling many feet below.

In a dark and boisterous world it was probably as well for travellers to hasten across the wastes of the moor. Cecil Torr in *Small Talk at Wreyland* relates how not far from Moretonhampstead on the eastern side of the moor a highwayman murdered Jonathan May in 1836. In July of that year two men, 'Buckingham' Joe (Oliver) and Turpin (Galley), were tried for the crime and found guilty. With commendable speed Buckingham Joe was hung in August, although there was some doubt whether the right man had been executed. He was felt to be a bad lot and deserved to be hung, so perhaps the execution reflected the nervous and basic state of society as much as justice.

At Lydford the justice had been just as summary, and it is perhaps significant that the last judge to preside over the Stannary Court was Judge Jeffreys. In 1795 Polwhele recorded that the president's chair, the jurors'

Oakhampton Castle & Town from the Park

were popular throughout the county. They were distinguished by their fineness of bone and skin although the dark red of the North Devons and the lighter, yellowy red of the South Devons were not 'commended by the eye of taste' as fitting into the landscape. There are still herds of these fine animals, which were at that time being selectively reared.

There was considerable variation in the kinds of sheep reared in different parts of the county, but no doubt the local Dartmoor ones would have been common in the Okehampton market. There were indigenous sheep, including the small and hardy Exmoor variety, and from 1800 the introduction of Leicester, Dorset and Southdown sheep and subsequent cross-breeding resulted in more numerous varieties than with cattle.

The parish church at Okehampton stood on a hill outside the town and in 1842 was burnt down, although the tower was saved and included in the newer Church of All Saints. A variety of bequests and parish lands allowed the poor to be cared for and the roads to be maintained. Each year the mayor who retired put forward two burgesses as candidates for mayor in the forthcoming year. This did not encourage a changing leadership: in fact between 1797 and 1820, just three men became mayor. John Colling alternated yearly with John Cadding between 1797 and 1811 and then with John Pleece until 1820. There was a guildhall in which meetings of the Council took place and a small prison.

To the south-east of Okehampton, the Taw rises near Steeperton Tor and flows through Sticklepath, west of South Zeal and South Tawton to North Tawton and beyond. Each of these were very small places although Sticklepath certainly had two mills in 1800 and a third by 1850, for corn, bone and woollen manufacture. Today water-wheels still turn here, one generating electricity for a private house. Another is used at the Finch Foundry, a working museum where horseshoes and scythes can be made. Originally a corn-mill then a cloth-mill, in 1814 it was taken over by Robert Finch and turned into an edged-tool factory producing agricultural and horticultural implements. Today its machinery runs unaltered. Recently new housing estates have been built in Sticklepath with some feeling for the traditional terraced stone and slate buildings that line the A30.

South Zeal, below the Exeter road, is a pleasant village which was laid out as a new town seven centuries ago with long narrow burgage plots, still there and clearly shown by hedge lines. There are some neat cottages, a number as old as the stone and slate Oxenham Arms, built in the fifteenth century. South Tawton has a few ancient houses grouped about the Church of St Andrew. Although, like South Zeal, it has modern buildings and wires to remind the visitor of the present century, each village feels pleasantly remote.

Around North Tawton, Itton Moor and Stone Moor were enclosed in the early nineteenth century and with them the wilderness which could scarcely have set the area south of the imposing mass of Cawsand Hill apart from the rest of Dartmoor. The wetlands of Devon were beginning to be drained by means of trenches four feet or more in depth with a stone gutter in the bottom, and by 1875 the danger to wildlife from unchecked drainage had already been recognized. In 1810 the quality of farms was being improved and the productivity of grassland becoming a byword. A few fields still sprout sedges and have patches of sogginess that were once common. These are the small reminders of the world of toads, frogs and newts which we have largely lost. Witches, who were invariably associated with these unfortunate creatures, stopped being persecuted after the execution of two women for witchcraft at Northampton in 1705, but superstitions surrounding them were strong in 1800.

The River Teign rises a few miles south of South Zeal and although not painted by Payne it was a great attraction to the early visitors to the county. It is possible to walk along it from Steps Bridge near Dunsford to Chagford, and to enjoy scenery not dissimilar to that described 200 years ago. Chagford, Drewsteignton and Dunsford are attractive places where the older properties are built of moorland stone and are roofed with thatch or slate. Perhaps Drewsteignton is the least changed with its fine Church of the Holy Trinity at one end of the square and the Drewe Arms, with no more than a front room for service and a hitching-post in front, on the northern side. Terraced houses complete the square and a road runs through its west side. Views from Drewsteignton across the deeply incised valley of the Teign are like many others around the moor, where trees, valleys and ranges of hills disappear into the distance. Castle Drogo, designed by Lutyens in the early 1920s, is an outstanding tourist attraction. This National Trust property, the last true castle, built of dressed granite blocks, stands above a steep hillside overlooking the Teign about 1½ miles west of Drewsteignton.

On an equally prominent knoll is St Andrew's Church at Moreton-hampstead, dominating the countryside to the east more than the town itself. In its porch are two gravestones to the memory of French officers who died in the town, presumably whilst on parole and billetted there with suitable families, as was the custom of the day. Both were lieutenants: Ambroise Quantin of the 44th Regiment of the Imperial Corps of Marine Artillery, who died in 1810, aged 33, and Armand Urbry of the 70th Infantry Regiment of the Line, who died in June 1811, aged 42. The fact that they warranted a burial and memorials of this nature suggests acceptance if not a liking for some of the prisoners in this small market-town. Here the buildings round the square and the older properties along the main streets echo those of 1800. An attraction for tourists was to visit the cromlech and logan stone on the other side of the river, or to ride to prehistoric Cranbrook Castle, overlooking the Teign about half way to Drewsteignton.

A little to the west of Moretonhampstead is the hamlet of Lettaford, which is typical of many ancient hamlets on and around the moor. It has two or three ancient medieval farm buildings including Sanders, which ten years ago was refurbished by the Landmark Trust. Buildings like Sanders or Stiniel at Chagford remained unchanged for centuries and were probably built in the mid-fifteenth century, with a cross-passage separating the farmer's living

Ivy Bridge

quarters from the shippen for cows. Later alterations often provided a separate entrance to the shippen for the cattle. In 1800 an occasional new house was built on the same ancient pattern, where the beasts would sleep under the same roof as the farmer. Even at this time he might sleep with his wife, children and any hired hands in a communal style if the house lent itself to this custom. After 1800 farmhouses tended to forsake this simple pattern and adopt a more modern one appropriate to privacy, although the use of granite and thatch was still favoured.

To the south of the moor Ashburton, with a population of more than 3000 in 1800, enjoyed the prosperity of a market-town, holding a weekly market for corn and other provisions near the Bullring in rather dilapidated buildings in the middle of North Street, which were replaced in 1849. Four annual fairs were also held, the one in March being particularly important for cattle whilst the November one specialized more in sheep. There were four corn-mills in the town which were kept busy by the farmers in the district. Farmers came from round about, as they did in other market-towns, to satisfy their own needs and to have an opportunity to catch up with the gossip of the market-place, perhaps also to visit the wheelwright or watch maker or have a pair of breeches made by the tailor. The town was self-contained and satisfied not only its own population but the numerous farms around.

Ashburton's prosperity depended to a small degree on tin and its position as a Stannary Town where mining disputes could be settled. It was the local centre for justice and returned two members to Parliament up to 1832, the voters being limited to freeholders, owners and also occupiers of the ancient burgage plots. After the Reform Act Ashburton sent only one representative on the basis of an enlarged franchise which in 1850 amounted to 200 voters.

The granite parish church of St Andrew stands above the rest of the surrounding buildings and is particularly attractive when seen from the bypass. Ashburton is a pleasant little town which has been rescued from the deadening influence of through traffic. Those living here can better enjoy both its shops and other facilities as well as the moorland slopes to the north of the town. Its pleasant domestic architecture is well preserved on West and East Streets, but rather spoilt in North Street, where part of a terrace was demolished to leave a grassed space. In 1830 there were already four Nonconformist chapels, and the Methodist chapel built in 1835 in the centre of the town imparts a classical dignity. Many of the granite and slate-hung buildings have survived, and recently the financial assistance of a town scheme has helped to keep the town attractive.

Ashburton was on the main Plymouth-to-Exeter road and, like Ivybridge, a favourite stopping-place. It had a good number of hotels and beer houses which thrived on passing trade. Just like other small towns it had a grammar-school, which here took the place of the old chapel of St Lawrence although the tower was kept. There was also a free school and various charities to help the poor.

Ivybridge also catered for travellers and was a place to which Plymothians went to enjoy a holiday or trip away from Plymouth. Its fame was based as much on the beauty of the River Erme, tumbling and roaring its way through this pleasant village, as on the old bridge that spanned it. Another bridge, sufficiently wide to take modern traffic, was built in the nineteenth century, leaving the narrow old stone bridge free from the wear of heavy modern lorries that rumbled through the town until the bypass was completed about ten years ago. During the past fifteen years Ivybridge has grown into a modern suburban town, with several pleasant early-Victorian buildings in the old main street and a pleasant valley that follows the river on its way up to the moor. Payne could well glimpse a picture of his own times if he were to look at the bridge and surrounding trees and vegetation now, and listen to the river dashing beneath.

A little to the east of the moor Chudleigh, with a population of about 1750 in 1800, was an old attractive market-town where most of the houses were built of cob and thatch. About a mile away, Ugbrooke Park was the home of Lord Clifford of Chudleigh as it is today. It is still a delightful property set in a secluded but attractive fertile valley. The house is quadrangular with two

Ugbrooke

Chudleigh Rocks

fronts and four towers, rendered and having battlements. It is opened to the public and a popular place to visit with its array of paintings and furniture. The park was about five miles round and was stocked with deer. The scenery is still varied and attractive with woods and lakes, rocks and chasms. In 1800 the largest trees were oaks and elms, which were interspersed with a variety of ornamental trees and chestnuts.

Close by, about a mile to the south-east of the town, was Chudleigh Rock, which rises imposingly in the landscape and can be seen from the main Plymouth road. Around it are other rocks and precipices and many people came from Exeter and elsewhere to picnic near its summit to see fine views over to Dartmoor. There were several beautiful parkland scenes within this rolling landscape, although today the increased building around Chudleigh Rock and new and improved roads have diminished its impact and reduced its attractiveness. Payne's delightfully romantic picture suggests a wilderness, that has now sadly been tamed, and a beauty rather more in sympathy with the feelings of the time, rather than the inhospitable wastes of Dartmoor. Today it is a favourite spot for climbers, and the woodlands about it and the rushing waters of Kate Brook keep the spirit of romantic beauty alive.

Just as the countryside has altered, so too has Chudleigh, where on Friday, 22 May 1807 a fire broke out in a baker's house. It was particularly fierce and caught the nextdoor house, in which were stored two barrels of gunpowder which exploded with a tremendous bang. The thatch of the nearby buildings was soon ablaze and the high winds which were blowing spread the fire throughout most of the town, except for some properties at either end. The fire-engine, which had been stored in the market house in Conduit Square, where the war memorial is today, was dragged out but was also burnt. Within three hours the market house and more than 166 houses in the town had been burnt down. The nearest fire-engines that might have helped were at Exeter, ten miles away, so little could be done. St Mary and St Martin's Church escaped and became a refuge for many of the homeless townsfolk.

The unfortunate victims had little to eat from Friday morning until Saturday, when a wagon loaded with bread and beer came from Exeter. The next day ready-prepared food arrived from the surrounding towns and Lord Clifford threw open Ugbrooke and sent food to those who could not leave the ruins. For some time at least the displaced townsfolk were able to use tents which had been sent from Exeter and camped around the town.

The generosity and understanding of people not only in Devon and Cornwall, where subscriptions were opened, but also in London was shown by £21 000 being raised to help those affected. The losses in the fire were estimated to total £60 000. By 1810 the town had almost been rebuilt, this time using brick and slate, and in accordance with an Act of 1808, setting the building lines sixteen feet back from the centre of the road.

At a time when the only building materials to be had were local ones, wheat-straw, or reed, was the cheapest Devonian roofing material and widely used. Some villages like Broadhembury and Gittisham in East Devon are still almost entirely thatched in the same way that Chudleigh and Honiton had been. At Honiton there had been fires in 1747, 1754 and 1765. The first had destroyed three-quarters of the town and the last 180 houses, leaving Honiton in a similar state to that endured at Chudleigh. Other towns like Crediton and North Tawton had also suffered fires, which were not uncommon and eventually resulted in building regulations being introduced.

Hartland to Bideford

Much of Devon's north coast is remote from the main roads and large towns, and has kept those rural qualities once common almost everywhere in the county. The grey slate rock of the Cornish coast continues ruggedly into Devon, running bleakly north from Welcombe to Hartland. The cliffs eastward between Hartland and Westward Ho! gradually attract plants and trees, so that between Blackchurch Rock and Portledge the lesser slopes of cliffs and combes are thickly clothed in oak, beech, ash, sycamore and silver birch. In the early nineteenth century there was a similar scene.

Beyond the sands of Westward Ho! and the entrance to the Taw/Torridge Estuary, are Braunton and Saunton. Over 600 acres of Northam Burrows and the pebble ridge are run as a country park, and nearby Saunton Sands are equally attractive and unchanged. Beyond Saunton dark-green and grey cliffs stretch eastward from Morte Point, past Ilfracombe, Lynton and Lynmouth into Somerset. The remote north-westerly parts of Devon in the early nineteenth century had poor access from the sea, and even worse roads.

Welcombe has probably changed as little over two centuries as anywhere in the county. It is a scattered village with a stone church that has a short square tower, and the Barton farm, with its strip of cobbled path from the modern road, situated no more than 100 yards away. About half a dozen loosely spaced houses stand near the Barton farm, which in most villages was the largest and most important farm. From the Church of St Nectan the surrounding hills form a valley to the west along the Abbey River, which runs down to Welcombe Mouth. The hills have few trees on them and in this part of Devon westerly winds give those that mature a blown and lopsided look. Next to the church is a small thatched cottage which by its diminutive scale

complements the church and could have been here in 1800. Only 220 lived in the parish then and there were not many more fifty years later.

White's Directory of 1850 lists nineteen farmers in the parish, plus beer houses run by John Parr and Thomas Prast. There were doubtless also labourers and odd-job men without a particular trade, but some essential needs may have required a trip to Hartland or Bude. The status of farmers depended on whether they were tenants or independent freeholders. Traditionally yeomen had land worth 40 shillings a year and a right to vote or serve on juries, and did not rely on the patronage of the lord of the manor as much as others. As late as 1910, when Joseph Rich Mugford of Mead in the parish of Welcombe was described on his tombstone as 'Yeoman', the distinction was still felt. He had been drowned at Marsland Mouth on 6 May, but his body was not recovered until 8 August, when it was washed up at Elmscott Cliffs. The pride and independence in this description was equally evident in 1836, when William Jewell's headstone was given the same inscription.

There were about 1500 townsfolk at Hartland in 1800 and in the next fifty years this number increased by 700. Hartland did not continue to grow and has remained an attractive little town with shops and businesses serving the farming communities around. In the past fifty years there have been the inevitable changes with new houses and small estates, but the town as a whole is little altered. The gradually curving Fore Street with houses and other properties, many either dating from or improved in Victorian times, has a variety of slate and white-painted cottages with different dormers, slight changes in alignment and the added interest of facing on to a raised pavement. Away from this pleasant street the houses are just as ancient and interesting.

In 1839 the market house, built of a dark rusty red stone, was converted to a chapel of ease, and it has a curious turret for a single bell above the porch. Around it, a number of the properties are ancient although some, like Perry House next to the Hart Inn, were built with regular and attractive fronts early in the nineteenth century. Harton Manor, like other buildings close to the chapel of ease, dates from Tudor times and has suffered different fortunes with different owners. It is interesting that its renovation from time to time has been recorded by plaques indicating various owners or builders through the centuries: IGP 1706, TSP 1819 and DLC 1977. In 1850 the town was in decay but now it has the neat feeling of a traditional market-town, neither opulent nor poor. It is certainly very pleasant in summer although perhaps the winter winds feel colder in this corner of Devon.

Three miles away is Hartland Point, with a modern lighthouse on the bold rocky coast. At Hartland Quay, a small jetty a little further south, coal, limestone and general goods were imported and local agricultural produce was shipped, including corn, although nowadays this seems to be a livestock area. Some time before 1790 there was a regular market at Hartland each Tuesday but after the turn of the century only two fairs were held here each year.

About a mile from the town was Hartland Abbey, but in 1799 Paul Orchard had the manor rebuilt on its site, incorporating only a few remains. In 1917 Lady Stucley of the new Hartland Abbey had some interesting fragments of the original stones of the Abbey Church placed in St Nectan's Church at Stoke. This church is about two miles from Hartland, set in a small cluster of ancient houses above a narrow-sided and beautifully wooded valley. Its 128 foot stone tower is visible for miles around and it has provided a landmark, particularly from the sea, from the time it was built in 1360. The church was modernized extensively in 1849/50 without destruction of the magnificent medieval rood-screen. As in many other parishes, it is likely that guidance and leadership came from the vicar, and in Devon, particularly during the nineteenth century, one clergyman often served the same parish for many years. Francis Tuffe (1755–1796) and William Chanter (1796–1859) gave continuity at Stoke for over 100 years between them.

It might be assumed that life at Hartland was uneventful with little to disturb the routine, but the parish records show that even without momentous action, there were all the normal human conditions and rivalries to be dealt with. One of the institutions that made decisions affecting the life of others was the local town meeting, which would have taken place annually and appointed a portreeve to act on the community's behalf in some respects. The parish accounts record that on 27 December 1784 this officer paid Mr Richard Thomas for 120 faggots of wood which were distributed to 52 poor people in severe snowy weather. Local justice as well as charity features in the accounts, with one shilling and two pence paid in September 1788 'to Rd.

Barnard for a scurge to whip Peter Way and whipping him', although no details of the unfortunate man's transgressions are given. Even in Hartland the effects of war and the Poor Law system were recorded:

1800	Dec. 2	Relieved a man with a pass	1 shilling 6 pence
		Relieved a man from a French prison with a pass to St. Ives	1 shilling
	Dec. 20	Relieved a soldier with a pass from a French prison.	1 shilling

Holsworthy to the south, and central to this wild north-western part of the county, also had a portreeve. The post continues there and is included in the town council as it is in Ashburton. These ancient positions and other old customs and rights were still being exercised in a variety of ways in different parts of Devon in 1800. Most of the responsibilities which had been in the hands of the lord of the manor and the local courts had now been taken over by the magistrates or county courts. But the remnants of power with which the lord of the manor held sway through its court baron, court leet, piepowder court and customary court were still felt. In Holsworthy the court leet was held once a year and was one of the oldest tribunals of common law, with jurisdiction over criminal matters. The court of piepowder was for settling disputes between itinerant tradesmen and their customers, whilst the customary court dealt with copyhold tenure where the title to land was held from the manorial roll. This type of tenancy was eventually abolished by the Law of Property Act in 1922.

There were also local weights and measures, and in the case of this town they were stamped 'Holsworthy Standard'. If false weights were used, it was the duty of the lord of the manor to punish the guilty in the court leet. The lord of the manor also fixed the price of bread and beer, and where bakers or brewers broke the law deliberately they could expect the customary punishment of being placed in the pillory, or the tumbrel or ducking-stool. Pillories were placed in the market square by the lord of the manor, but were abolished by statute in 1837 and rarely used after 1815, whilst the ducking-stool was last used in England in 1809.

The parish stocks came under the jurisdiction of manor courts and can often be found stored away as an object of interest, possibly in the church or churchyard or in a local museum, in a number of Devon parishes. This centuries-old punishment, inflicted more to wound the dignity than anything else, is reputed to have last been used in Holsworthy in 1861, the same year as the last public hanging took place in England. Elsewhere the stocks were still used in the 1870s. Another rural relic often found today is the pound for straying cattle, and most villages had one in use at the end of the eighteenth century.

Clovelly is a particularly fascinating village set on a hillside above a stone quay and descending along a narrow cobbled village street built in giant steps and negotiated for centuries by pack-horses or donkeys. The last of the houses are at the rear of the beach itself, and the cliffs and hills around are densely wooded. Travellers at the turn of the eighteenth century remarked upon the houses being stepped one above the other, and whilst seeing over their neighbour also receiving smoke from its chimneys. This has not changed although perhaps more coal was burnt and modern heating reduces the pollution. The main part of the village, built facing directly on to the downward cobbled way, is neatly uniform, with grey slate and white or pastel shades everywhere. Different windows, eve levels, doors and balconies, combined with a gradually bending street which ensures some shelter from the wind, create a picturesque village.

At the top of the street is a fountain, of a modest nature, provided in 1901 by Christine Hamlyn 'to honour the memory of a great Queen' (Victoria). The street itself could well be a monument to the early nineteenth century, if not in every detail, totally in spirit. The Hamlyns have been the lords of the manor since the eighteenth century, when Zachary Hamlyn built Clovelly Court close to All Saints' Church, about a mile from the village. Later Sir James Hamlyn planted and laid out the Hobby shortly before his death in 1829. At that time fishing and farming sustained the parish, and this has changed little, although a growing number of retired people enjoy its beauty.

Clovelly and Westward Ho! were made famous by Charles Kingsley, whose father was rector at Clovelly, but it was not until later in the century that they started to attract many sightseers. Buck's Mills, on the coast between, is no more than a pleasant scatter of houses in its own valley but has its own small beach and limekilns for limestone brought by coastal craft. In recent years a good proportion of the ancient cottages have been purchased as holiday homes, as they have elsewhere.

Beyond the sands of Westward Ho! and Northam Burrows, which must have been very sparsely used 180 years ago, but today swarm with holiday-makers in the summer, is the mouth of the Taw/Torridge Estuary. It is the only major estuary on the north coast of Devon and indeed the only major estuary in the largely rugged length of coastline which extends 100 miles from the Camel Estuary in Cornwall to the River Parrett in Somerset. Before meeting at Instow, the Taw and Torridge flow through wide shallow valleys up to the towns of Barnstaple and Bideford, respectively.

In 1724 Daniel Defoe on his tour of Great Britain described these as 'two great trading towns'. He remarked that whilst Barnstaple was the older, Bideford was more flourishing, and was 'a pleasant, clean, well built town'. The ancient quay and buildings alongside it had been supplemented by a new spacious street, Bridgeland Street, which Defoe rightly said was as broad as Exeter's High Street. Its wealthy merchants were trading to all parts of the world, and had a large trade with Ireland, importing wool and yarn which was then sold to the serge makers of Tiverton and Exeter. Barnstaple shared this trade 'and in the herring fishery, and in a trade to America, if Bideford cures more fish, Barnstaple imports more wine, and other merchandise'. In some aspects at least, the ancient rivalries between these two attractive towns continue, but not in overseas trade.

Bideford's ancient bridge of 24 spans was once built of wood, but in 1535 it was rebuilt in stone, incorporating the old oak timber. Its condition and narrowness when seen by Defoe encouraged some people to wait until the tide was out and cross over the sandy river bed. By 1778 there was worry about its stability with the increased use by carriages, since it had been built for pack-horses with recesses for people on foot to avoid them. Between 1795 and 1810 the carriageway was widened to nine feet and pavements two feet wide provided. The parapet walls were rebuilt and recesses on the cut-waters made larger. The two medieval chapels by the bridge, dedicated to St Mary the Virgin and All Saints, were removed during the next thirty years, also to make way for traffic. The further widenings and rebuildings in 1925 and 1968 have left this remarkable bridge a worthy feature of the town and infinitely more attractive than the new concrete bypass bridge downstream, which promises to destroy the scale of the town and estuary by its overbearing mass when completed. It was, however, widening of the bridge between 1795 and 1810 for the better use of wheeled vehicles rather than pack-horses that signalled the transformation from old Bideford to new.

There were only 3000 inhabitants in 1800 whilst today the sprawling suburbs rising above East-the-Water and behind the town towards Northam house 12000. Bideford still has a market-town atmosphere, and the ball-clay coasters loading at the quay introduce movement and thoughts of distant lands. It has always been this way in Bideford, and during the Napoleonic Wars boatbuilding was strenuously undertaken. Sloops of war and several frigates were built at the ten shipyards in the vicinity and the manufacturers of cordage, rope and sails prospered. Amongst the ships built was the sloop *Cornet*, with sixteen guns, which served along the Spanish coast in 1808, taking *La Sylphe* and helping to spike the guns of two forts near Santander. Others from Bideford had similar success. There were several tan yards, and leather goods were made, as too was common earthenware pottery. There was a rope-walk between Bridgeland Street and the Strand, and there were breweries, an iron foundry and limekilns.

The war with the United States at the end of the eighteenth century temporarily stopped a thriving trade in tobacco, which had been so large that Bideford imported more than London. By 1850 it had revived, however, and timber, hemp and tallow were imported from the Baltic and America, wines and fruit from Spain and Portugal, cattle from Ireland, coal, culm, iron and flagstones from Wales, and marble and slate from Cornwall. The effects of the wars on the town seem to have been slight, and the Newfoundland trade revived. Ships of up to 300 tons reached the bridge and smaller vessels travelled up to Weare Giffard and later used the Torrington Canal to reach Torrington. The quay at Bideford was very much smaller at the turn of the eighteenth century than it is now. In 1828 and 1842 substantial improvements were made to it to help port traffic, and this was the responsibility of the lord of the manor, who claimed ownership and dues from it.

Bideford had 67 vessels registered and 256 seamen employed in 1800, and

Tapley — Mr Clevelands — & Appledore, from the Wear

grew in importance by 1850 to have 150 ships. The danger of the press-gang during the war years no doubt worried townspeople but five years before, in 1795, there had been an even more disturbing requirement of ship owners, by which the Government expected them 'to furnish able bodied men for the navy; an able bodied seaman being accepted as equivalent to two able bodied men'. The following were required from each port: Barnstaple 74, Bideford 48, Dartmouth (plus Brixham) 394, Exeter 186, Ilfracombe 49 and Plymouth 96.

Bideford's 'volunteers' would also have come from other towns like Appledore, three miles away in the parish of Northam and with a population of a little more than 2000. Appledore has always been divided into East and West Appledore with the Church of St Mary, built in 1838, standing between them. In the first half of the nineteenth century the population increased by 80% and early-Victorian architecture is common in the older parts. Six-panelled doors and sash-windows were in vogue for both old and new houses, and today Appledore is a fascinating labyrinth of narrow passages and courts with delightful views across the estuary to Instow and Braunton Sands. A comparison of Payne's picture of salmon fishermen and the older part of the town by the river with the scene today shows how the hillside has been developed since then, and also how its beauty has endured. The modern covered shipyard, whilst depressingly obtrusive, keeps alive shipbuilding and the camaraderie of a working town.

Appledore's houses are built tightly together and when some years ago a tactless health inspector suggested forty were unfit for human habitation, meaning that the Housing Acts required some modernizations, this almost caused a riot. The seafaring folk of Appledore showed a vigorous community spirit, which needed considerable tact to calm. In the remoter parts of North Devon settlements have kept a community spirit lost elsewhere but as fiercely independent now as it was 200 years ago.

At Northam nearby, the Church of St Margaret stands close to a small square and has a number of narrow roads and ancient houses around it. There are more modern bungalows and houses than the village deserves, and it is hardly separated from the modern development of Westward Ho! Views across Northam Burrows under a blue sky and a warm sun are stunning, though, and probably as attractive as they were two centuries ago.

Before the reforms of the 1835 Municipal Corporations Act, Bideford claimed the status of a borough and was administered by a mayor, four aldermen and ten capital burgesses, with a recorder, two sergeants at mace, and other officers. The insignia of Bideford included two greater and two lesser maces. The greater maces were repaired in 1812 by the mayor, Stephen Wilcock, who also had arched crowns added. A silver oar had been held by the lord of the manor, John Clevedon, but this was passed to the new corporation when it purchased the manorial rights in 1881.

If the bridge at Bideford was an asset, the Bridge Trust seems to have been an even greater one. For centuries the Trust had held land and property to allow it to maintain the bridge, which it did with money left over. It also supported the grammar-school, which was held in a room belonging to the Trust. The school had its own land to pay for the schoolmaster and other requirements. A farm of 57 acres in West Buckland provided rent, and a wood of 20½ acres in the hands of the trustees yielded £204 in 1799 and £439 in 1813, possibly reflecting the inflated wartime prices which benefited all owners. In 1817, £420 was paid for a house in Bridgeland Street for the schoolmaster, who was expected to teach his charges Greek, Latin, history, geography, astronomy, mathematics, etc. He took three boys free of charge, who were nominated by the trustees, and the cost of others had to be less than £6-6s per annum. In 1825 a national school for about 200 children was built at the expense of the Bridge trustees.

In addition to supporting the school, the trustees provided for fire-engines, relieved the poor, repaired the guildhall and paid for the bridge wardens, hall keepers, etc. Later, in 1841, they appropriated a field of 1½ acres as a public cemetery, half to be used by the established Church. The Anglican Church of St Mary was an ancient fourteenth-century building which had been extended and altered at various times. Except for the tower it was rebuilt in 1865. Amongst the Nonconformists were the Quakers, whose Great Meeting House was built in 1696 and was very well supported in the early part of the nineteenth century. In 1815 a Wesleyan chapel was built in Bridge Street and the Baptists also had a chapel in the town.

The market is still held and at the turn of the eighteenth century its activities encroached on to the quay from the market-place. The town was well supplied with foodstuffs, and fairs for cattle were held in February, July and November. The use of the quay for market trading continued through the first half of the nineteenth century, during which time, in 1825, the first paddle steamer built in Appledore, named *Torridge*, called here. It did good trade taking passengers to Bristol and London. In 1826 the quay was lit with the first lights in the town and a decade later gas-lamps were gradually introduced for the winter months.

Bideford's charter gave wide powers of imprisonment, and it had three prisons and a gaoler. It was not until 1837 that the first police officer, Elias Palmer, was appointed on a yearly basis to superintend the watchmen of the borough who had undertaken the policing before.

Ten miles south of Bideford, Torrington occupies an enviable position on top of a hill above the Torridge, and because of the acres of common land between the river and the town, as well as on the hills to the east, it has kept its attractive setting. Below the town Taddiport Bridge spans the river close to the Torrington Creamery. There is a pleasant stone toll-house by the bridge and some older buildings along the road uphill away from the town. The road into the town from Taddiport skirts upwards across the common and before reaching the centre passes a number of terraced Victorian houses, which can be seen from the south like those in Payne's painting.

When Torrington was visited by Payne it was still a market and

Torrington

wool-manufacturing town, and at the turn of the century the Staple Vale Woollen Manufactory was built on about 50 acres of common land. The rent and money due for the renewal of the lease were used to pay for the apprenticing of poor children. There were common rights for the poor on 300 acres of land at Hatchmoor, Western and South Commons. The town also had the benefit of rents from town lands which in 1815 were conveyed by Lord Rolle, who had held them in trust, to the mayor and 22 other trustees. There were 136 tenants in 1850 and they could hold their property for a basic period of three lives, with the possibility of renewing the lease on payment of a sum at the time of surrender. Their rents were used for the benefit of the poor and to maintain the church, guildhall and other public buildings. The modern guildhall is a neat stone and brick building which stands on piers jutting into the market square and was built in 1865. Close by is the Pannier Market in South Street, built, according to the weather-vane perched above a decent pediment on a small turret, in 1842. The square is made more attractive by the Black Horse Hotel, which probably dates from 1681, the year on a plaster panel above a fireplace inside.

There was once a castle in Torrington but by 1800 it had long since disappeared, although bowls were played where it had stood until the fruity language of some players annoyed someone in authority and led to play being stopped for a number of years before the turn of the eighteenth century. The game was later revived and there is a green there today. The ladies of the town raised funds for an obelisk which was put up on common land to the south of Torrington to commemorate Waterloo in 1819.

There are several properties of distinction in or near the town. Beam House, which was a seat of the Rolles about a mile from the town on the Bideford road, is now used for a school and is situated by the Torridge in a most delightful setting. Palmer House, built by Sir John Palmer, is another building of distinction close to St Michael's Church on the main road. It was visited by Dr Johnson and Sir Joshua Reynolds, who was John Palmer's brother-in-law. Its façade has brick ionic pilasters and is quite handsome, although the garden at the rear has been built on. Number 28 South Street was built in 1701 and has some attractive plasterwork including a fine plaster-moulded hooded porch. Torrington remains a pleasant market-town, larger but still seemingly self-contained and with the added attraction of the Dartington Glassworks on the industrial estate.

Barnstaple to Lynmouth

Back at Bideford, the modern houses of Ethelwyne Brown Close along the waterside in East-the-Water, over the bridge, show that modern development can fit in and be attractive. On the way to Barnstaple, Instow, situated at the confluence of the Taw and Torridge, has a delightful view across to Appledore and along the estuary to Braunton. Only 340 people lived here in 1800, enjoying good fishing and farming, although numbers had nearly doubled by 1850. There is a fine cricket ground with a thatched pavilion overlooking the estuary, which a latter-day William Payne would find irresistible. Cricket started in Instow in 1823, the North Devon Club being one of the oldest.

The approach to Barnstaple along the estuary in 1800 was dominated by a very attractive stone bridge. Most of the buildings at that time were on the north-east side of the Taw and it was not until later in the nineteenth century that development spread out from the old centre near the castle mound. The town was only slightly larger than Bideford in 1800 with a population of 3700, although a further 1300 or so lived in Pilton and the suburb of Newport, which was included in the parish of Tawstock. In 1835 the Municipal Corporations Act extended Barnstaple to include both areas.

In the early nineteenth century Barnstaple was more akin to Bideford than it is today. At that time both depended on trading through their respective quays and the prosperity of their merchants. In Barnstaple, Queen Anne's Walk on the west side of the main quay was an exchange for the merchants. It is used now by elderly people as a rest-room, but once it resounded to the bargaining of merchants selling their wares, unloaded at quays which could take vessels of between 100 and 200 tons. Small barges could continue up river for three miles before discharging their cargo. Some sand barges still use

Barnstaple from Sir Bouchier Wrey's

the River Yeo and the remaining quays but they are peripheral to the working life of the town. The principal quay is now a bus lay-by and the waterfront is mainly used as a pleasant walk with views across to the timber yards opposite or along the river to the sixteen-span stone bridge.

Until the last part of the eighteenth century, woollen goods called duroys, tammies, serges, shalloons, baizes, flannels, plushes, etc., were shipped from Barnstaple. Following the war this type of export diminished and by 1820 different trade was sought, although several blanket- and serge-mills remained in the town. Goods from the Baltic, France, Spain, Portugal and North America were imported and trade increased after 1822, when bonded warehouses were established. The unhindered coastal trade included imports of coal, timber, iron, groceries, spirits and freestone, sending out grain, wool, bark, leather, paper, etc. On Sunday, 22 July 1822 the *Lady Rodney* steam packet arrived at the quayside in Barnstaple and started sail's decline.

In 1800 Barnstaple had 73 vessels registered and trading from it, totalling 5387 tons and employing 326 men. Although there was a shipbuilding industry at Barnstaple no outstanding warships seem to have been constructed. However the *Weazle*, a sloop under the command of the Hon. Captain Grey, set sail from here on the evening of 10 February 1799. She had been stationed at Appledore for some time so the captain and crew were well known. After she had left the shelter of the estuary a storm blew up and the sloop was wrecked at Baggy Point. All the 105 crew and one woman were drowned, only one of the crew who had been left behind on shore remaining alive. Naval ships were accustomed to having women aboard even when going into action. They often acted as cooks, although later Chinese cooks found favour.

There were quays and a dock at Penhill or Fremington Quay below the town where some boatbuilding took place and the larger vessels could more easily load and unload. The picture of Heanton Court and the tower of Heanton Punchardon Church beyond was probably painted from Penhill, and the schooner shown making for the bar could well have been one of the larger trading vessels. There were breweries, people making woollen goods, brushmakers and ropemakers in Barnstaple. The important pottery industry, centred on Potter's Lane since medieval times, continued to export to the various colonies as it had since the sixteenth century.

Before the Improvement Act of 1811, which allowed the borough to improve street frontages and a number of medieval practices, Barnstaple must have been an insanitary place and perhaps rather more antiquated and picturesque than today. There was a multitude of Tudor and medieval buildings jumbled together with eaves jutting out over the streets and throwing rainwater on to those below. The cobbled streets sloped steeply towards the middle and formed a channel for all manner of refuse to be washed away by the rain. The smells from the dung pits attached to the houses must have been overpowering. Added to this, they were cleared out and their contents removed whenever it was convenient. The butchers placed their stalls along the High Street, flanked by massive chopping blocks, together with whatever was needed for their trade. Amongst the noise and confusion of trading, and the rough roads, some unfortunates tumbled headlong into the mire.

The Act encouraged the owners of antiquated properties to modernize them, and Gribble in his *Memorials of Barnstaple* recorded that in just one part of the High Street with 68 houses on either side of it, 24 properties were rebuilt and a further 25 were either refronted or modernized to look like new shortly after 1811. Some properties like the Three Tunns public house were left largely unaltered, but during the period up to 1830 there were great changes not only in the High Street but also to the rear of it. The town expanded rapidly over the first fifty years of the century reaching 8600 inhabitants, and many terraces were built to the south and east of Boutport Street and the High Street. Many of these areas have been cleared away although both the High Street, and Boutport Street where the old cattle market was held still keep the buildings and frontages built at that time.

A year after the Improvement Act had been passed the butchers' market was built, housing 34 shops in a double line running from the High Street. In 1826 a handsome guildhall with the borough coat of arms in its pediment was built in a Grecian style over the entrance to the butchers' market, and above the market was a corn exchange. The market hall was rebuilt in 1855 and the attractive shops in Butchers' Row opposite carry on the tradition. The cast-iron work and neat shops are a delightful feature of the town centre. Changes as radical as those of 1811 may shortly introduce a larger scale and so weaken the very fabric of a town that is in essence a Victorian market-town.

The quarter and petty sessions were held in the guildhall, whose offices are now used by the town council and voluntary organizations. At the turn of the eighteenth century the stocks and cage were still in use and the prison was in a cramped two-roomed building which in 1828 gave way to a larger and better one. It was the town constable and two beadles who kept the peace until the introduction of a police constable about 1836.

Ebberly Place was a much admired conversion undertaken by Henry Hole after 1817. The building had been cavalry barracks during the war and had been sold by the Government. Bideford had quartered the Devonshire Regiment in 1799, encamped in Drum Field, but Barnstaple seems to have had a more permanent army presence, with the 58th Regiment of Foot stationed there in 1798. There were no major fortifications built at either Barnstaple or Bideford.

By 1826 most of the town had been repaved, and the central dip in the road in the High Street and elsewhere had been filled in. All the principal streets and some in the outskirts had oil-lamps in 1826, although as at Bideford, the lamps were used only during the winter months. With new flagstones placed along the streets as they were improved, life became considerably less hazardous and closer to modern convenience, although some streets like Bear Street kept their cobbled paths for some time.

Heanton Court on the Taw

In addition to the Friday market, where corn and all kinds of provisions were sold, there was an annual fair which started on 19 September and lasted several days. It was one of the best in the country for horses and cattle and was one of the largest for both business and pleasure. The festivities included a ball held at the assembly room and a stag hunt which started on the border of Exmoor. The theatre, normally opened for three days weekly from September to Christmas but rarely well patronized, was open every day during this fair. In addition there were four great cattle markets each year.

The parish church of St Peter is now quite central and surrounded by ancient almshouses that introduce a calm antiquated feeling in a bustling market-town. Before 1800 it was rather closer to the eastern edge of Barnstaple, and a grammar-school was held in a building in the churchyard. The Blue-coat Schools were reformed in 1834 but were much older institutions, and later national schools were built for a much larger population.

Pilton was still independent of Barnstaple until 1835, and this part of the town still feels like a village. St Margaret's stands at the top of a sloping street, above some stone almshouses, and some of the nearby houses are clearly of Tudor origin.

The Wesleyan chapel which was built in Barnstaple in 1815 was, like many others, a thriving hub of Christian belief and energy. The Nonconformists were also represented by Independent and Presbyterian congregations, who united towards the end of the eighteenth century and built a new chapel in 1839, and by the Baptists, who after 1824 met in a chapel in Vicarage Lane. Christian charity was as strong here as in other towns in the county and evident in charities and almshouses. From around 1815 friendly societies were set up to encourage thrift, and in the 1820s the North Devon Infirmary and the Dispensary in Boutport Street were built, providing medical help for those living in North Devon.

To the south of the town the river winds up a beautiful wooded valley to Bishop's Tawton, which was a small village about three miles from Barnstaple. It faces across the valley to Tawstock House, which was substantially rebuilt after a fire in 1785. An ancient gateway remains and the house is now used as a private school. Below it is St Peter's, Tawstock, which has some of the best family monuments in Devon, mainly to the Bouchier and Wrey families. The beautiful parkland around the house has matured from the time Payne captured its beauty, but the view of Barnstaple from Sir Bouchier Wrey's grounds has changed with new building.

On the other side of Barnstaple, Ashford, on the hillside above the Taw, has recently grown to be a commuter village while Heanton Punchardon has modern houses on the ridge. But the wide shallow river and its sandbanks are still a marvellous wildlife reserve. Different grasses and flowers grow in profusion, visiting curlew, oyster-catchers, redshank and dunlin rest there, and seagulls and other birds soar above. The river was famed for the great quantities of salmon that swam up it, and fishermen still net them.

Braunton Parish covers 10000 acres of different types of countryside and had a population of about 1200 two centuries ago, which more than doubled over the next fifty years. The streets around the parish church of St Brannock are narrow with the oldest buildings in the village bordering them. Like other attractive places in Devon, Braunton has spread greatly and only the efforts of local people have preserved this pleasant spot. One particularly interesting feature is the Braunton Great Field of 350 acres divided the same way it was in medieval times.

All the features of a medieval open field – the furlongs, headlands, strips and bond stones – are vividly painted on the landscape by different types of crops. It is one of the most productive pieces of land in the area, giving heavy yields of cauliflowers, cabbages and leeks as well as cereals and hay. Cattle and sheep are still occasionally put out to pasture in the Great Field although the traditional practice of throwing the whole field open to stock after the harvest disappeared long ago. With the diminished width of headlands and lanchards, the traditional home of rats, the Field is freer from vermin. Other traditional practices like spreading seaweed for fertilizer have also gone.

Many villages in the late eighteenth century had vestiges of the ancient open fields worked by villagers with shared ploughs and oxen. Braunton Great Field's headlands and dividing strips of land have become narrower and the farmers working it have become fewer. No more than five major farmers own most of the strips whereas a century ago there were more than sixty owners. Goodwill and public opinion should help keep this heritage, but the number of strips fell from 491 in 1889 to 140 in 1975. Elsewhere in the county during the eighteenth and early nineteenth centuries, common land was being enclosed by planting hedges and building stone walls, so that access to the countryside as well as the type of farming and use were beginning to change. Open fields gradually became consolidated in blocks of land as local agreements converted strips into fields enclosed by hedges. Many of the hedges that have been lost over recent years were those of the late eighteenth century, although the enclosure movement spanned 200 years or so. Only at Haxay in Humberside and Laxton in Nottinghamshire are there open fields to compare with Braunton Great Field.

South of the Great Field, the marshes represent agricultural progress. Early in the nineteenth century Charles Vancouver visited Braunton while preparing a report for the Board of Agriculture and suggested they should be reclaimed. The local landowners commissioned an engineer, James Green, to prepare a scheme, and an Act of Parliament to allow enclosure was passed in 1811. The scheme included the construction of a massive bank, the Great Sea Bank, to reclaim 945 acres of marsh. Work was completed between 1811 and 1815 at a cost of about £20000 using labour from Cornwall, Ireland and Holland to supplement local workers.

Strict rules for management of the reclaimed marsh were laid down and marsh commissioners and inspectors appointed. The toll-house near Sharper Marsh, towards the north end of the bank, was built for a marsh inspector.

Tawstock

Ilfracoomb

After reclamation some of the marshland was sold to pay for the enterprise but the main salt-marshes were divided to recompense some 130 claims for common rights. Farmers from the village were awarded fields in the southern part near Flat's Pill. Manorial tenants were similarly rewarded but the tithe to their plots was the property of the lord of the manor and the land reverted to him after 99 years. Care was taken to group the lord's lands and the results can be seen in the larger 15 acre fields.

Some arable crops were grown on the reclaimed Braunton Marsh, but eventually the area became used almost entirely for grazing. The former marshes are now said to be some of the best beef-fattening land in the South.

Each of the holdings had its stone barn or linhay where cattle might shelter and where fodder could be stored above. There were about forty of these buildings evenly spread across the marshes but most have now collapsed, although recently a scheme for restoring one or two and rebuilding the dilapidated walls has been undertaken.

In most parts of the county the normal ploughing of pastures and use of fertilizers over the past thirty years has imported a greenness that up to 1939 was unusual. During the last century it was probably unknown. The countryside would have had an abundance of flowers found now only in some roadside verges, hedgerows and odd fields here and there. Fields in permanent pasture held their own variety of flowers according to drainage, soil and slope and changed with the seasons. Equally, all manner of wildlife was more common. The Large Blue, a butterfly that until a decade ago lived on the cliff lands in North Devon and is now extinct, would have been amongst insects large and small which in their turn made good pickings for the birds. The Victorian era when a summer's day was alive with the vibrant noise of the countryside has almost gone. The price of plastic opportunity and two world wars has been the destruction of superabundant wildlife. The hedgerow trees, grown for use in all kinds of implements, furniture and buildings for a much smaller population, have often been felled and fewer trees left to grow. Cobbett complained of the increase of conifers and the loss of seasonal changes in colour and varied form.

Braunton Burrows and Woolacombe Sands in 1800 were barren and unknown as attractions except to a few local people. Like Westward Ho! they developed only after 1850. The small villages of Georgeham and Mortehoe were tiny communities with ancient houses and at Lee, between Morte Point and Ilfracombe, a few fishermen and farmers lived isolated lives on the rocky coast. Rugged cliffs up to 800 feet high jut into the sea along the north coast, and rough tracks crossing them rose and fell so steeply that the traveller found it best to lead his horse. The cliffs have always had trees and grass growing in crevices as well as precipitous rocks of grey, green and darker hues, with impressive strata and folds.

In 1800 Ilfracombe had changed little since Defoe's time. There was a plain neat church and the town was built along a single street, with the irregularity of age. In spite of the differences in height and width of the buildings, most travellers thought it was a good place with its shops and well paved streets. It had an excellent sheltered harbour with land on three sides and protected on the fourth from sea and wind by a huge rock which stretched half way across the mouth. There was sufficient space for vessels to seek shelter here when unable to enter the Taw/Torridge Estuary, as well as to carry on the normal coastal trade. The population was about 1830 at the beginning of the nineteenth century and grew slowly, by a hundred each year, until about 1850, then rapidly increasing by an average of a thousand people per year up to 1900.

Ilfracombe was very popular with those who enjoyed picturesque countryside with contorted cliffs, hills, woods, rocks and water. The quay from which Payne painted the harbour had been rebuilt in 1760, and the anchor he depicted is not unlike one there now. The pier has been extended and widened, the first time in 1828, and is now used for car-parking, although the chapel overlooking the harbour mouth is still used as a lighthouse marking its narrow entrance.

One of Ilfracombe's more famous sailors was Rear-Admiral James Bowen, who was born there in 1751. He was employed in the merchant navy in the Africa and West Indies trade, then served on the *Artois* at the battle of Dogger Bank in 1781. The action resulted in £213 000 being paid in prize money for ships and French stores, plus £5 for each of the enemy killed or wounded. The admiral received about £2000, captains £1400, lieutenants £109 and ordinary seaman £4. The agent for sale of goods was James Bowen, who made £10 000 as a result. After a distinguished career and successful actions as well as three years' convoy service between 1799 and 1803, for which the East India Company gave him silver plate valued at £400, he became Commissioner of the Transport Board, and in 1809 he supervised the re-embarkation of the Army at Coruna. In 1816 he became a Commissioner of the Navy, and remained one until he retired in the rank of rear-admiral in 1825. He died at the age of 84 in 1835.

The highway from Barnstaple passed over bleak uncultivated moorland which was later enclosed but at the start of the nineteenth century must have seemed inhospitable and difficult to cross. It had only a narrow rough track unsuitable for heavily loaded brakes and four-horse coaches. In July 1816 the Revd B. Woolocombe, describing travel in and around Ilfracombe, recorded 'all wheel conveyance at that time was done by donkey-chairs, and very proud and dignified their occupants looked, as turning their heads first to one side of the way and then to the other as they proceeded slowly along the streets and lanes of the place, and had a deliberate look at all they passed'. The big event of the day was the three-horse mail travelling through from Barnstaple.

By 1830 Ilfracombe was attracting visitors from Barnstaple for outings and they could have watched the fishing boats, a West Indiaman passing along the Bristol Channel or a battleship. Before the stationing of a lifeboat at Ilfracombe three large skiffs cruised in the winter to help ships in distress.

Perryn Harbour nr Ilfracoombe

There were more than seventy vessels registered at the port and there was a considerable herring industry, although the only export was oats.

By the end of the century the few houses close to the harbour had increased and terraces had spread impressively above the harbour and up the hillside. The cast iron which was fashionable then is a pleasant reminder of the railway age when most of the building took place. Amongst the earliest terraces were Hillsborough, above the harbour, Montpellier Terrace and Marine Terrace.

Along the coast from Ilfracombe is the small village of Berrynarbor, beautifully painted by Payne, who labelled the picture 'Perryn Harbour'. The stone tower of St Peter's Church stands proud above a neat group of stone and slate houses. It is on top of a knoll which is hemmed in by rounded hills but open to Combe Martin Bay. There is a lych-gate and a cobbled path runs past slate gravestones, some at rakish angles, which mark the passage of time like pages from the parish history book, while above the tower a weather-vane shaped like a fox runs with the wind and reminds the casual visitor this has always been hunting country.

A short way further east from Watermouth Castle, built in fanciful mood in 1825, is the straggling village of Combe Martin. Its houses stretch back up the valley for a mile or so from the pleasant sandy cove edged by rocky cliffs. The Church of St Peter served a parish of 800 at the turn of the eighteenth century and 1440 fifty years later. The steep hillsides with trees and pastures yielded silver in Elizabeth's reign but attempts to win silver in 1800, 1813 and 1817 were not profitable, although attempts from around 1837 until 1875 were.

Coal ships and fishing smacks were the main vessels coming to the remote coast, where pilots for the Bristol Channel could be taken on. The market had been discontinued in the eighteenth century so that those living here were mainly dependent on fishing and farming until the mines reopened, although hemp was grown about the town and shoemakers' thread spun from it. A free school was founded in 1733 and rebuilt in 1820, for 40 children.

From the sea Combe Martin looked like a deep narrow gulf with magnificent cliffs rising on either side. The richness of the valley was a marked contrast to the dark cliffs, which were softened only by grass that grew on their ledges and gentler slopes. The whole of this coast from Ilfracombe has a profusion of headlands and rocks, which to the east of Combe Martin include Great Hangman and Little Hangman, rising menacingly from a boiling sea that breaks across their rocky base. It is hardly any wonder that the townsfolk talked of 'a good wreck season' as cheerfully as they might have referred to 'a good mackerel season'. Just as in South Devon, to plunder a wreck thrown on the rocks was not robbing but winning from the sea.

The magnificent scenery around Combe Martin introduces the superb cliff scenery and rolling hills of Exmoor. North Devon has always been well stocked with sheep, and the wind-swept heights and wooded valleys of Exmoor are well suited for this type of farming as well as the traditional stag hunting. Amongst the great attractions for intrepid adventurers in this remote

Coomb Marton

area was the Valley of Stones. In September 1789 the Revd John Swete enjoyed the different type of scenery where the tops of hills were crags 'taking the shapes of disparting towers, gigantic obelisks and a thousand other fantastic forms'. With a glimpse of the sea and the wind-swept barren feeling of the hills and heathland, it was an obvious subject for any painter, and Payne's view, seen now from a modern car-park, has scarcely altered.

Ideal subjects too were Lynton and Lynmouth, which in 1800 started to attract visitors. These two little villages were part of a larger parish with 480 people living in it. In 1802 an artist called T. W. Williams drew Lynton and showed the parish church of St Mary with its square tower and eight or nine cottages in the community. The village lay in a hollow and enjoyed some shelter although the countryside was rocky and bare. Later, in 1817 and in 1833, the small parish church was enlarged to satisfy the rapidly growing population, and houses spread around it.

Below this small group of houses in 1800 was Lynmouth, which was no larger and included some sheds and pits where herrings were cured. Just as at Ilfracombe, the sea provided villagers with a living, supplemented with a little

Valley of Stones

Linton

Linmouth

smuggling. In the eighteenth century it was recognized that there were only two sides, the government excise officers and the rest of the community, who willingly enjoyed smuggled goods.

By 1820 there was a scatter of houses on either side of the River Lyn as it dashed down to the sea. Development was quite rapid at the beginning of the century but the biggest changes around the villages took place between 1850 and 1860 with enclosure of common land. Until this time the hills around Parracombe, Lynton and Lynmouth were nothing but acres of gorse and the roads were dangerous and at times impassable. Later the pack-horse trails were widened to make roads suitable for carts and carriages.

Devastating floods occurred in 1952 when the East and West Lyn Rivers, which flow through beautiful wooded valleys and converge before running through Lynmouth, became raging torrents after several days of continuous rain. The rivers eventually burst their banks and swept away 28 bridges and destroyed 93 houses in and around Lynmouth, changing the course of the River Lyn. New car-parks and rebuilt houses have changed this picturesque holiday resort, which beneath its layer of postcards and holiday souvenirs is still a pleasant place. More recently Lynmouth has been paved for pedestrians and cars excluded, so that the pace of life has been slowed a little towards that of 200 years ago.

Index